EARLY HISTORY OF VAISHNAVISM IN SOUTH INDIA

EARLY HISTORY OF VAISHNAVISM IN SOUTH INDIA

BY

S. KRISHNASWAMI AIYANGAR

GYAN

Published by

GYAN

Gyan Publishing House
5, Ansari Road
Daryaganj, New Delhi-110002
Phone: 011-47034999, 9811692060
E-mail: books@gyanbooks.com

Distribution Network
gyanbooks.com
India, USA, Canada, UK, Australia

ISBN: 978-93-6208-063-9 (PB)
First Published, 1920

2nd Impression 2024

Printed at: Gyan Press, Delhi.

EARLY HISTORY OF VAISHNAVISM IN SOUTH INDIA
Author: S. KRISHNASWAMI AIYANGAR

EARLY HISTORY OF VAISHNAVISM IN SOUTH INDIA.

EARLY HISTORY OF VAISHNAVISM IN SOUTH INDIA

BY

S. KRISHNASWAMI AIYANGAR, M. A.,

Professor of Indian History & Archaeology & Fellow of the Madras University; Member of the Royal Asiatic Society of Great Britain & Ireland; Fellow of the Royal Historical Society; Professor & Sometime Fellow of the Mysore University; Reader, Calcutta University.

THE OXFORD UNIVERSITY PRESS.

LONDON, NEW YORK, TORONTO, MELBOURNE, BOMBAY AND MADRAS.

1920

Inscribed

to

His Excellency

the Right Honourable Sir Freeman Freeman Thomas,

Baron **WILLINGDON** *of Raton,*

G.C.S.I., G.C.I.E., G.B.E.

Chancellor, University of Madras

as a token of the author's great esteem

for

His Excellency's kindly interest and enlightened sympathy

PREFACE

THE following lectures, presented to the public as the fourth course of Madras University Special Lectures in the Department of Indian History and Archaeology, formed the subject on which I intended to send a paper to the International Congress of Orientalists, which was to have been held at Oxford but for the outbreak of the War. It was suggested as worth doing as the result of a discussion on the subject which I had with Sir George Grierson, who at the time was interesting himself in the subject. He wanted more of Vaishnava literature should be made known to the European public and suggested the translation of Yatindramatadipika, a manual of Vaishnavism, and the Arthapanchaka of Pillai Lokacharya. The translation work has been done since, by my friend Mr. A. Govindacharya of Mysore; and the historical part of the subject was awaiting study for various reasons, among which other occupation was the principal contributary. The timely appearance of Sir R. G. Bhandarkar's treatise on "Vaishnavism,

Saivism, and Minor Religions" made the taking up of the subject more urgently necessary. In a review of the work in the Journal of the Mythic Society, Bangalore, I indicated that I would work up the subject so as to bring to bear upon the question all the light that may be got from sources recently made available. I took advantage of the occasion offered by the First Oriental Conference at Poona, over which Sir R. G. Bhandarkar himself was to have presided but was unfortunately prevented from doing so by illness at the time. The objection was made in certain friendly quarters that it was highly improper that I should have taken up a controversial subject like this and presented a paper to a Conference held in honour of Sir R. G. Bhandarkar himself, "*criticising his views.*" The word criticism conveys a little too often unfortunately, the sense of finding fault which is far from the accepted significance of the term. Criticism is of the essence of historical research and no one is justified in proceeding on research work without making sure that the footing gained already by previous work is actually beyond cavil. That can be done only by a thorough re-examination of the work already done, not with a view to find fault or exhibit shortcomings only, but to take stock of what has been satisfactorily established and what cannot equally satisfactorily be so regarded. Without such an examination it would be assuming too much to proceed further in research work. It is in that view that the work was undertaken, and I had not the slightest doubt, nor do I cherish the least touch of it now, that Sir R.G. Bhandarkar himself would welcome such a re-examination. It is not want of respect for him that prompted the work; but much rather the wish to complete the work that he has done in a subject in which such work as he had done had to be done by him at a great disadvantage. I have no doubt whatsoever that this investigation will be received in the spirit in which it is offered, as a critical study of an interesting question, by Sir R. G. Bhandarkar himself. I would appeal to other friends who may chance to read the book to consider any criticism in the book in the spirit of the most friendly investigation of the position of other scholars with no further object than the evaluation of actual achievement. I cannot conclude this prefatory note better than by making an extract from one of the most eminent recent authorities on the subject of History, Lord Acton :—

"For our purpose the main thing is not the art of accumulating material, but the sublimer art of investigating it, *of discerning truth from falsehood*, and *certainty from doubt*. It is by *solidity of criticism* more than by the plenitude of erudition that the study of history strengthens, straightens and extends the mind."[1]

To avoid clumsiness in print transliteration in the body of the book has been given up. The necessary and the correct pronounciation is given in the index which the reader is requested to consult in cases of doubt or difficulty.

I am grateful to His Excellency Lord Willingdon for kindly according permission to my inscribing this course of University Lectures, the first to be published by me since His Excellency's assumption of office as Chancellor of the University of Madras, to him as a slight token of my esteem for his sympathy for oriental research.

I am obliged to Mr. B. R. Srinivasan the Proprietor of the Tata Printing Works, for the neatness and expeditation with which he put the work through the Press.

MADRAS UNIVERSITY.
25th January 1920.

S. KRISHNASWAMI AIYANGAR.

---

1. Study of History. p. 40.

University of Madras

Madras University Special Lectures: Fourth Course.

Early History of Vaishnavism in South India.

Lecture I.—Vaishnavism, what it is—the subject—the stage reached by research work upon this by previous work—Sir R. G. Bhandarkar's work 'Vaishnavism, Saivism and minor Religions' in the Encyclopædia of Indo-Aryan Research—Alvars and Acharyas previous to Ramanuja—Sir R. G. Bhandarkar's views—his general position—Recognised order.

Lecture II.—The specific question of Alvar Kulasekhara—his age—evidence upon which Sir R. G. Bhandarkar bases his conclusions—evaluation of the evidence—another similar view—who was Kulasekhara—evidence of his own works—at what period we may have to look for him—evidence of literature and inscriptions—chronological order of the Alvars.

Lecture III.—Was Nam Alvar the last of them all?—Arguments in support of this position—other views—general position of this Alvar—his works—the name Tiruvaymoli and its explanation—the school of Bhakti—Saivism looked upon as collaborator—Tiruviruttam and Tiruvaymoli—Other Alvars, particularly Periyalvar—evidence of his works—probable age.

Lecture IV.—The first Alvars—their general position and works—Poygaiyar and Poygai Alvar identical—posibility of two Poygaiyars—possible contemporaneity with Tondaman Ilam Tirayan—Tirumalisai Alvar—His Pallava contemporary—Evidence of secular literature—other criteria of age—Paripadal—position of Vaishnavism—effect on general position in regard to Sanskrit literature and history of Indian culture.

EARLY HISTORY OF VAISHNAVISM IN SOUTH INDIA

LECTURE : I.

VAISHNAVISM: WHAT IT IS

At the outset of a course of lectures on Vaishnavism it will be expected that the term Vaishnavism should be defined. It will be equally clear to everybody that anything like a definition of the term Vaishnavism should be difficult unless a small treatise is written upon the subject. Like most other religions of India Vaishnavism has a Philosophy and Religion of its own. As a philosophy it bases itself upon the Upanishads and is acknowledged by scholars to be, in certain respects at any rate, a more faithful and closer rendering of the upanishadic teaching. As a religion it reaches its roots into the Tantra. Its religious ritual therefore, is of the Agamic or Tantraic character in general.

Its philosophic character is Upanishadic. To give merely a practical notion of what is to be understood by Vaishnavism I might say here that Vaishnavism regards Vishnu as the supreme being with Sri or Lakshmi in close association with him. It has its own tenets, which for the sake of brevity might be given in the following text of a contemporary writer of the life of Ramanuja. "With Lakshmi I am supreme; my conviction is difference (or duality); surrendering oneself into the hands of a preceptor is the most secure way to salvation; holy thoughts on the eve of death unnecessary; salvation to a believer certain. At the present time Mahapurna (Periya Nambi) is the guru to be sought."[1] These are the words in which God directed Ramanuja to the acceptance of his mission when at the critical moment he vacillated, harassed by doubt whether he was equal to the burden of the propagation of the gospel of Vaishnavism. The fundamental idea of Vaishnavism is contained in one verse of

---

1. Śrīmān param tattvam aham, mattam mē
bēdaḥ prapattir nirapāya hētuḥ |
nāvaśyakicha smṛti rantyakālē
mōkshō, Mahāpūrṇa ihāryavaryaḥ | |
Āndhrapūrṇa's Yatirājavaibhavam' Sl. 40.

Tirmalisai Alvar, which may be freely rendered :—" Let Your Grace be for me to-day ; let it come to-morrow ; let it wait still longer and come sometime after ; Your Grace, I am sure is mine. I am certain, O! Narayana, I am not without you, nor are you without me. "[1]

It will thus be seen that both in its philosophical and in its ritualistic aspects Vaishnavism reaches back to the same antiquity as other Brahmanic religions, and on a question of origins, it will be found that there is very little to choose in respect of priority and posteriority. Vaishnavism is the direct offspring of the school of *Bhakti* as 'Saivism is, and it seems to me that Vaishnavism diverged from Tantraism definitely in its early association with the Vaidic philosophy. It is not my purpose to discuss this aspect of the subject, my concern being the history of Vaishnavism. Sir R. G. Bhandarkar has shown in his book " Vaishnavism etc " that the school of *Bhakti* so called is traceable to the age of Buddhism and Jainism.

---

1. இன்றாக நாளையேயாக இனிச்சிறிதும்
நின்றாக நின்னருளென்பாலதே — நன்றாக
நானுன்னையன்றியிலேன் கண்டாய் நாரணனே
நீயென்னையன்றியிலை.

Nānmukan Tiruvandādi 7.

This might be regarded as the legitimate orthodox development of the orthodox Madhyadesa at a time when the ferment of dissatisfaction and free thought on the Upanishads led on in the East to the protests of Jainism and Buddhism against Vedic ritualism. Its history in northern India is traceable in its main lines at least from the 5th century B. C., but our concern here is the history of Vaishnavism in the south.

THE SUBJECT.

The history of Vaishnavism in South India came in for attention as a subject of study while yet that eminent Tamil scholar and philologist, Bishop Caldwell, was actively working in the field of the history of the literature of Tamil. In the course of his investigations he arrived at, to us somewhat strange, conclusion that Vaishnavism was the foundation of Ramanuja more or less It is nothing strange since he regarded the Augustan age of Tamil literature to have been in the 13th century of the Christian era and later ; but what is still more strange is that the late professor M. Seshagiri Sastriar, the first Indian occupant of the chair of Sanskrit and Comparative Philology in the Presidency College, should have held the same view and stated specifically that the Alvars were disciples of Ramanuja. The error in the case of Caldwell arose from his finding the Centum on Ramanuja included in the *Prabandham*, 4000. That excuse cannot be held to justify the view of the Indian professor. Since then investigation on the subject has advanced many stages, and many scholars have worked in the field with, more or less, of success. There were often controversies, enlivened occasionally by a certain amount of acrimoniousness, and certain conclusions were made possible notwithstanding this particular feature. The late Mr. Sundaram Pillai could not find any history in the Vaishnava traditions, and there were not wanting scholars who went to the other extreme of argument, and would deem it hardly necessary to subject these traditions to a critical examination at all. This latter school is ably represented by Mr. A. Govindacharya whose work, the "Divine Wisdom of the Dravida Saints", embodies the traditional account. Some of my younger friends submitted theses on this subject for their M. A. degree examinations of which a few were published. My attention was particularly drawn to this subject by an article on the " Age of Manikkavasagar " contributed by the late Mr. L. C. Innes. As became a late eminent judge of the High Court the article dealt with the main thesis with a very large number of *obiter dicta* scattered about the article on various matters of vital interest to the literary history of Tamil, a part at any rate of the history of Vaishnavism came in for some observation, which drew my attention. At about the same time the late Mr. Gopinatha Rao was writing a history of Vaishnavism in the pages of the Madras Review. The essential part of it he repeated very recently in his Sir Subrahmania Iyer Lectures delivered before the University of Madras. During recent years Mr. M. Srinivasa Iyengar, M. A. devoted a considerable space to this history in his learned work ' Tamil Studies '. Professor Rajagopalachariar of the Law College, Madras dealt with the subject but not from the historical point of view essentially. Meanwhile Pundit M. Raghavaiyangar dealt with the history of some of the Alvars in the Sen Tamil with his usual learning.

The culmination of this series of efforts upon the history of Vaishnavism was reached in Sir R. G. Bhandarkar's " Vaishnavism, Saivism and minor Religions". This was published by the veteran orientalist as a part of the Encyclopaedia of Indo-Aryan Research. The first part Vaishnavism attempts to deal with the whole history of Vaishnavism from the beginning which the learned Doctor finds in the period co-eval with the rise of Buddhism and Jainism, if not earlier. It is this classical work on the subject that challenged my attention as the learned scholar quoted from me when he reached the history of Vaishnavism in South India, and offered some criticism of my work. He agreed with me that the Alvars and Acharyas were previous to Ramanuja and should be looked for in that particular period; but he questioned my views in regard to the traditionally recognised order in which these are mentioned. This criticism naturally called for a re-examination of my position with the fulness that the great reputation of the venerable doctor and his learning alike demanded. It is therefore necessary to state his views more fully and exhibit his general position before proceeding to examine them carefully.

The Bhagavta itself states in book XI, Ch. V that Vishnu assumed different forms in the first great periods of time, and describes the different modes of worship of Him. For the *Kali* age he has simplified even the ***agamic*** worship of the previous age to the extent of offering salvation to those who would devote themselves to him without even subjecting themselves to the discipline of acquiring spiritual knowledge and practising *Vairagya*, (not giving way to the desires of the flesh). In order the more effectively, to achieve His object of saving the people of this earth He will come into this world, according to the Purana, in ten avatars of His, different from those of the previous æons of time. His real devotees will be found scattered here and there in the whole of Bharatavarsha, but they will be found in large numbers in the Dravida country on the banks of the Tamraparni, the Vaigai (Kritamala), the Palar (Payasvini), the Kaveri and the Mahanadi flowing west (that is, Periyar) It is in this favourable spot that He would descend to do the work of salvation.[1] In the land of Tamra-

1. Kalau khalu bhavishyanti Nārāyaṇaparāyaṇāh
kvachit kvachit Mahārāja Draviḍeshucha bhūriśaḥ !!
Tāmraparṇī nadī yatra Kritamāla Payasvini
Kavēri cha mahā puṇyā pratīchu cha Mahānadi !!
Yē pibanti jalam tāsām manujā manujēsvara
prāyō bhaktā Bhagavati Vasudēvē amalā'sayāh !!.

parni was born Nammalvar and Madhurakavi ; in that of the Vaigai, Periyalvar and his daughter Andal ; in that of the Palar, Poygai Alvar, Bhudattalvar, Pey Alvar and Tirumalisai Alvar ; in that of the Kaveri, Tondaradippodi, Tiruppan Alvar and Tirumangai Alvar ; and in that of the Periyar, Kulasekhara, if his birth place was Tiruvanjikkulam in the state of Cochin. This citation would make the Bhagavatam a work posterior to the age of the Alvars, but it is possible that this chapter is a later interpolation. Granting that it is, it ought to have been interpolated long before Vedanta Desika, as he quotes the passage as authority for certain of his positions in his work Rahasyatrayasaram. It would be an interesting enquiry in itself to compare in detail the Prabandha works and the Bhagavatam. That work will have to be left over for the present. What is to the point in the history of Vaishnavism in this citation is that *Bhakti* gets associated with the south, almost exclusively as it were, though even here its connection with the Agama and Tantra is clearly indicated.

In regard to this however, it would be just as well to call attention to what the Padma

Purana has to say regarding Srimad Bhagavatam and how it actually came into existence. In the course of his interminable peregrinations sage Narada happened to be in the vicinity of Gokula on one occasion when he saw a young woman in distress in a desert tract with two elderly men lying apparently dead near her. The sight of the sage put some heart into her to appeal to him to solve to her the riddle that brought her to her then distressful condition. She said she was born in the Dravida country, had her early growth in the Karnataka and flourished to some extent in the Maharashtra. She proceeded thence to Gujarat with her two sons when life became difficult for her. As she moved further from there life to her was becoming gradually impossible; but she kept trudging on as best she could till she came to where she actually was at the time. When she touched the ground on which she then stood, she was suddenly transformed into the youthful woman she was while her two young sons were grown old and withered, ultimately falling dead as she thought they were.

Sage Narada pondered a little while and then addressed the young woman like one who knew it all. He said that she had no cause to distress herself. She was *Bhakti* (devotion) and her two little ones were *Gnana* (spiritual knowledge) and *Vairagya* (negation of desire). In olden times even *Bhakti* required the assistance of these two auxiliaries for the attainment of salvation; but in this age of Kali, *Bhakti* alone was quite enough—the more so when she was actually in the ground hallowed by the feet of Lord Krishna as a child. Hence the death of her children who were mere superfluities for her purpose. The points worth noting in this story for our purposes is that the Dravida country was the land of birth of *Bhakti* which flourished to a gradually diminishing extent in the Karnataka, Maharashtra and Gujarat.

Whatever may be the source which the Purana quoted above might have taken its information from, it is actually found that the Alvars and Acharyas of the Vaishnavas as well as the Adiyars of the Saivas were people born in the Tamil country, all of them exclusively, and propagated their gospel there. Dr. Bhandarkar has given satisfactory evidence of a very much earlier and a northern origin for the cult of *Bhakti* and there are evidences of its prevalence in the centuries preceding the Christian era in the region of "the middle country" in northern India. We shall show presently that the inspiration, for Vishnu *Bhakti* at any rate, came from the north. The school of *Bhaktas* in the Tamil land elaborated and worked it up with features characteristic of Tamil culture and sent it back in a more realistic reflex wave which swept over the whole land of India. We shall now proceed to the history of this school of Vaishnavism in the south.

VAISHNAVA TEACHERS OF THE SOUTH.

The Vaishnava teachers, accepted as such among the Vaishnavas of South India, fall into two broad classes, the Alvars (saints) and the Acharyas (teachers). The successsion of the latter began some five generations before Ramanuja and is a continuously growing list in respect of each section, nay each family, of the Vaishnavas of the South. The other class is by common consent anterior to this and more holy according to the recognised "guru paramparas". They are twelve in number and fall into three clases, as arranged in Sir R. G. Bhandarkar's work under reference. The list which is in the order of the dates given in the "guruparampara", may be quoted here for convenience.

ANCIENT.

Saroyogin	....(Poygai Alvar)
Bhutayogin	....(Bhutattalvar)
Mahadyogin or Bhrantayogin..	....(Pey Alvar)
Bhaktisara	....(Tirumalisai Alvar)

MIDDLE.

Sathakopa	....(Nam Alvar)
Madurakavi	
Kulasekhara	
Vishnuchitta	....(Periya Alvar)
Goda	....(Andal)

LAST.

Bhaktanghrirenu	....(Tondarappodi Alvar)
Yogivaha	....(Tiruppan Alvar)
Parakala	....(Tirumangai Alvar)

Then follows Sir R. G. Bhandarkar's comment which I quote in extenso ;

"The date of the first ordinarily given, is B C. 4203 and of the last, B. C. 2706, and the others range between these two. Not only are these dates fanciful, but even the sequence shown above is unreliable. Krishnaswami places the last in the earlier half of the 8th century A. D and all the preceding ones impliedly before that date but there is distinct evidence to show that Kulasekhara flourished much later. He was a king of Travancore, and one of the works composed by him styled Mukundamala contains a verse from the Bhagavata Purana (XI, 2, 36). Again in an inscription on a tablet existing in a temple at Naregal in the Dharwar district, translated by Dr. Fleet, [1] it is stated that Permadi of the Sinda dynasty vanquished Kulasekharanka, besieged Chatta, pursued Jayakesin and seized upon the royal power of Poysala and Dhorasamudra, the capital of the Poysala dynasty. In another inscription, [2] this Permadi is represented to be a vassal of Jagadekamalla II, whose dates range between A. D. 1138 and 1150. While the former was in power as Mahamandalesvara, in the seventh year of Jagadekamalla, *i.e.*, in A. D. 1144, a certain grant was made by a body of sellers of betel leaves and nuts. The Kulasekhara mentioned as being vanquished by this Permadi, must be a prince reigning on the western coast as the others, Jayakesin, the Kadamba prince of Goa,

1. J. Bo. R. As. Soc. XI. 244.
2. Ibid page 251.

the Hoysala king [1] and so forth were. Putting this statement and the quotation from the Bhagavata Purana together, it appears highly probable that the Alvar Kulasekhara lived in the first half of the 12th century. The sequence therefore, given above cannot be implicitly believed in. Still it may be admitted that the earliest Alvars flourished about the time of the revival of Brahminism and Hinduism in the north, which extended up to the Mahratta country, as we have shown from inscriptions and antiquarian remains, and must have extended still farther to the south. The earliest Alvars may be placed before, about the 5th or 6th century, but there is nothing to show that Vaishnavism had not penetrated to the Tamil country earlier, that is, about the first century. But an impetus such as the rise of the Alvars indicates could in all probability come only from the energy of the revival.

" The hostile relations into which the Alvars and the Saiva saints, Nayanmars, came with the Buddhists and Jainas, lend support to the view we have advocated." In this

---

1. It is doubtful if the Hoysala power ever reached the coast at this period.

criticism of the venerable Doctor there are three points that emerge into relief :—

(1) that Alvar Kulasekhara lived sometime about the middle of the 12th century A. D.

(2) As a consequence the order in which these Alvars are usually named is unreliable.

(3) That the earliest Alvars must have flourished about the time of revival of Brahminism and Hinduism in the north, and therefore about the fifth or the sixth century A. D. while the possibility is admitted that Vaishnavism might have penetrated to the south as early as about the first century A. D.,

THE VAISHNAVA TRADITION.

We shall proceed to examine these three positions in the order in which they are enumerated above. In regard to the whole of this position it has to be remembered that Vaishnavism is a living religion with a very considerable following and a continuous tradition so that even tradition in a matter like this has to be given some weight historically, though we are not entirely dependent upon tradition alone in regard to this subject. The works of these Alvars are composed in the vernacular of the country, Tamil, and was collected and thrown into the form, in which they have come down to us by oral tradition as well as in written form, in the latter days of the lifetime of Ramanuja himself. The ***Prabandha*** "***four thousand***" includes in it a centum on Ramanuja himself by one who called himself Amudan of Arangam (Srirangam), and who declares himself, in the course of the work, to be a disciple of Ramanuja's chief disciple Kurattalvan.[1] He refers to these Alvars in that work in a particular order, but places Nam Alvar, the last of them all for which there is a particular reason which we shall notice presently.

The order is :[2]

1. Poigai Alvar.
2. Pudattalvar.
3. Pey Alwar.
4. Tirupanalvar.
5. Tirumalisai Alvar.
6. Tondaradippodi.
7. Kulasekhara.

---

1. **Rāmānuja Nūrrandādi St. 7.**
மொழியைக்கடக்கும் பெரும்புகழான்வஞ்சமுக் குறும்பாம்
குழியைக்கடக்கும்நம் கூரத்தாழ்வான் சரண்கூடியபின்
பழியைக்கடத்து மிராமாநுஜன் புகழ்பாடியல்லா
வழியைக்கடத்த லெனக்கினியாதும் வருத்தமன்றே.
2. **Ibid Stt. 8-17.**

8. Periyalvar.
9. Andal.
10. Tirumangai Alvar.

The name of Nam Alvar, with that of Madurakavi, is omitted. The former comes in for more elaborate reference in the verses immediately following.[1] While we may not be warranted in assuming any strictly chronological order perhaps from this, we ought to grant that it is the recognised general order of precedence in point of time as there is no other kind of order known or recognised among the Vaishnavas with the solitary exception of the position of Tiruppan Alvar. The exception in the case of Nam Alvar comes in for a satisfactory explanation as he is the only one among the Alvars who figures in a succession of religious preceptors proceeding from one's own particular guru right up to Vishnu himself,

---

1. Ibid, Stt. 18—19.

எய்தற்குறிய மறைகளை யாயிரமின் தமிழால்
செய்தற்குலகில் வரும் சடகோபனைச் சிந்தையுள்ளே
பெய்தற்கிசையும் பெரியவர் சீரையுயிர் களெல்லாம்
உய்தற்குதவும் இராமாநுஜன் என்னுறுதுணையே.
உறுபெருஞ்செல்வமுந் தந்தையுந் தாயுமுயர்குருவும்
வெறிதருபூமகள் நாதனும் மாறன் விளங்கியசீர்
நெறிதரும் செந்தமிழாரணமேயென்றிந்நீணிலத்தோர்
அறிதரநின்ற இராமாநுஜன் எனக்காரமுதே.

the chief Guru of them all.[1] It is this pre-eminence of Nam Alvar [2] that is responsible for this particular work removing him out of his place and treating of him in a number of stanzas immediately following. As against this order might possibly be quoted a sloka from Pillan, the disciple and immediate successor in the *apostolic seat* of Ramanuja to whom the latter entrusted the work of commenting on *Tiruvaymoli* 1000, the work by pre-eminence[3] of Nam Alvar. He sets all the names in one single sloka [4] and gives the names of only

---

1. Adhikārasangraha of Vēdāntadēsika St. 3.
என்னுயிர் தந்தளித்த வரைச்சரணம் புக்கி
யானடைவே யவர்குருக் கணிரைவணங்கிப்
பின்னருளால் பெரும்பூதூர் வந்தவள்ளல்
பெரியநம்பி யாளவந்தார் மணக்கால் நம்பி
நன்னெறியை யவர்க்குரைத்த வுய்யக்கொண்டார்
நாதமுனி சடகோபன் சேனைநாதன்
இன்னமுதத் திருமகளென் றிவரைமுன்னிட்
டெம்பெருமான் திருவடிகளடைகின்றேனே.

2. Ses. note 1, p. 18 above.
Rāmānujanūṛṛandādi 18.

3. Stanza 19 noted under note 1, p. 18 above.
Rāmānuja Nūṛṛandādi 19.

4. Bhūtam Saraścha Mahadāhvaya Bhaṭṭanātha
Śrī Bhaktisāra Kulaśēkhara Yōgivāhān
Bhaktāngḥrirēṇu Parakāla Yatīndramiśrān
Śrīmat Parānkūśmunim praṇatosmi nityam.

11, omitting Andal. The exigencies of versification perhaps would not warrant the inference of any chronological order. It must be noted in this connection that the Tamil poems of Kulasekhara are included in the collection which received the sanction of Ramanuja.

VEDANTA DESIKA'S ARRANGEMENT

Vedanta Desika the great scholar, teacher, and controversalist, who lived through almost the first three quarters of the 14th century and who in a Tamil *Prabandham* of his own has a chapter on those that are entitled to "communion with God", makes, in the first stanza of this section, a recital of the names of these Alvars omitting those of Andal and Madhurakavi. The first four are mentioned in the usual order, then comes in Satakopa and then follows Vishnucitta; immediately following him is Kulasekhara, then follows Yogivaha, then follow Bhaktanghrirenu and Tirumangai Alvar. Madhurakavi is mentioned in the next following stanza as the man who first taught that God's communion is attainable only by means of a "preceptor" (guru), and his work included in the *Prabandham* is one of 11 stanzas which state that he had made his choice of a *guru* in Satakopa, and that therefore his salvation was certain to him. In regard to the order here again, the exigencies of writing in verse is to be considered because all the names are brought in in one stanza of the poem, whereas the first work above referred to names each one in a separate stanza. The following stanza of the work of Vedantacharya we discuss, contains "the order of preceptors" referred to in the previous paragraph and this stanza is recited by the Vaishnavas of the *Vadakalai* section at the commencement of every serious holy act of theirs. The order is given beginning with one's own preceptor, and then passes on to the succession of preceptors advancing backwards from the nearest. Passing over the succession of *gurus* on this side of Ramanuja, it begins with Ramanuja, then comes in his principal preceptor Periya Nambi, then his preceptor Alavandar, then his preceptor Manakkal Nambi then his master Uyyakkondar, then Nathamuni, then Satakopa, then Visvaksena (Senainathan), then Mahalakshmi and then Vishnu Himself. In this it will be noticed, as soon as the first *Acharya* is reached he passes on to only one of the Alvars, Satakopa and then passes out of the earth into heaven itself.

This arrangement is what exactly detaches Nam Alvar from the group of the Alvars in the arrangement of Amudan of Srirangam.[1] That ought not to be interpreted as it has been at any rate in some quarters done, as arguing the posteriority of Nam Alvar to the other Alvars. In a consideration of the question whether there was any recognised order of precedence in chronology, the valid source of information is the one first quoted above, namely the order indicated in the poem Ramanuja Nurrandadi of Amudan of Srirangam. We shall return to it later.

---

1. See stanza quoted above in note 1, p. 19.

LECTURE II.

SPECIFIC QUESTION OF ALVAR KULASEKHARA

KULASEKHARA'S LIFE ACCORDING TO THE GURUPARAMPARA

According to the ordinarily prevalent accounts in the Vaishnava guruparampara Kulasakhara is regarded as the incarnation of *Kaustubha* (the jewel in the breast of Vishnu), and was born in the year Parabhava, the month Masi in Tamil, (Sans. Magha) Friday the 12th of the bright fort-night and Nakshatra Punarvasu. He was born according to this authority in the "city of Kolli (Quilon), otherwise Tiruvanjikulam". He is said to have been the son of a king by name Dridhavrata. After the usual education he was installed as ruler. Early in his career he became attached to the Vaishnava school of *bhakti* (devotion) and was particularly interested in having the Ramayana read out to him. In the course of this reading he became absorbed in it so much that on a particular occasion when they read out the portion where Rama marched forth single-handed against the great army of

Khara and his two brothers he called out in his abstraction and ordered the whole of his army being put in motion to the assistance of Rama. The reader understanding his position went through the rest of the story rapidly and brought it to its termination bringing Rama victorious back to the hermitage where Sita was, and then Kulasekhara is said to have felt relieved. On another occasion it would appear his ministers wanted to wean him of this extraordinary devotion to Vishnu and brought about the loss of some jewels and valuables left in the sanctum of his palace, access to which was denied to everybody else excepting to himself and to the few Vaishnava priests engaged in service in it. When the responsible officials charged the Vaishnavas with the theft he is said to have affirmed " no Vaishnava will ever commit such an enormity", and, in token of his faith in them, to have thrust his right hand into a pot into which was put a malignantly poisonous cobra. When the cobra did him no harm and his court felt satisfied that he was right they ceased to interfere with him. His devotion to Vishnu grew stronger day by day till at last he gave up royal life, went forward to Srirangam to be "perpetually" in the divine presence. It is there that he is said to have composed his Mukundamala his Sanskrit work, and the larger portion of the "Perumal Tirumoli" in the Tamil *Prabandham*. At the instance of Ranganatha himself he moved forward to Tirupati taking Kanchipuram on the way. He has one ten relating to Tirupati. He returned from Tirupati and travelled on to various Vaishnava places till he came to Mannanarkovil (in all probability, Kattumannarkovil in the South Arcot district) where, while in his devotion to god he is believed to have given up mortal life. His whole life is said to have been not more than 25 years. This account makes it clear that the hagiologists knew almost nothing about his life except perhaps his place of birth. Even in regard to that, there is apparently an error. The guruparampara makes Kolli and Vanjikulam two names of the same place. We have already pointed[1] out that Vedanta Desika in the

1. பொன்புரையும் வேற்குலசேகரனே மாசிப்
புனர்பூசத் தெழில் வஞ்சிக் களத்திற்றோன்றி
அன்புடனே தம்பெருமான் செம்பொற் கோயில்
அணைத்துலகின் பெருவாழ்வு மடியார் தங்கள்
இன்ப மிகு பெருங்குழு உக்காணமண்மே,
விருளிரிய வென்றெடுத்த விசையிற்சொன்ன
நன்பொருள் சேர்திருமொழி நூற்றைந்து பாட்டும்
நன்றாக வெனக்கருள்செய் நல்கிநீயே.

Prabandhasaram Stanza 8, mentions his place of birth as Vanjikulam while Kulasekhara himself states that he was ruler of Kolli. The guruparampara seems merely to attempt at a solution of the inconsistency in these two statements by the simple expedient of equating the one name with the other. Unless, as was pointed out above, Vedanta Desika had the specific knowledge that Kulasekhara was born in Vanjikulam though he was king of Kolli, we ought to accept Kulasekhara's statement that he was a native of Kolli ; while the other is certainly very probable, as the Bhagavata account specifies Periyar among the rivers hallowed by the birth of *Bhaktas.* The astrological details that are given are apparently the work of the hagiologists and are of no value historically as they must have made a backward calculation, if they at all did so, to suit their own particular dating. Of the real details of his life this biography gives nothing.

THE AGE OF KULASEKHARA

Proceding now to an examination of the age of Kulasekhara the extract quoted above makes it clear that it is the opinion of the venerable scholar, Sir R. G. Bhandarkar "that the Alvar Kulasekhara lived in the first half of the 12th century." It will also be remembered that this conclusion is arrived at specifically on the consideration of two inscriptions which mention a Kulasekharanka, and which refer themselves to the Chalukya emperor Jagadekamalla, A. D. 1138—50. More generally, however, he has been led to this position by fixing the latest limit for Kulasekhara in the Madhvacharya, Ananda Tirtha who flourished about A. D. 1199 to 1278. The downward limit is fixed as the date of composition of the Bhagavatapurana which this Acharya regarded as sacred and quoted as authority. Sir R. G. Bhandarkar therefore would place it two centuries earlier than Ananda Thirtha on the ground that "it cannot be very much older, for its style often looks modern and in copying from the older puranas it falls into mistakes, such as the one pointed out by me in another place [1]." Kulasekhara's posteriority to the Bhagavata is also sought to be established from a citation which the learned doctor found of the *sloka* of the Purana, XI, 2, 36. That Kulasekhara was later than the Bhagavata may be

---

1. See Bom. Gaz. Vol. I, part ii, page 164 for the reasons.

provable ; but this citation from the Bhagavata-purana I do not see in the southern editions of the Mukundamala accessible to me. A Kannada edition, a Grantha edition and a new edition which was published sometime back in Devanagari, none of them show this *sloka*. There is besides the fact that this particular *sloka* is recited in apology for any shortcomings in the performance of religious acts commonly, at the end of almost every religious ceremony so far as I know. It will be admitted therefore that some editions of the Mukhundamala might bring it in at the end; but even so it is not found in the southern versions known to me. The citation referred to therefore loses its decisive character. That apart this chronological position can easily be demonstrated impossible. The period A. D. 1,100-1150 is exactly the period in which the *Prabandham*, 4000 must have been cast into the present form by Ramanuja, at any rate with his sanction, and the Ramanuja Nurrandadi incorporated into it gives an honourable place to Kulasekhara as an Alvar. Most of these separate Prabandhas and their authors are given commendatory verses which are generally recited before beginning the recital of the particular *Prabandha* concerned. The part of the *Prabandha* of Kulasekhara Alvar is introduced by verses in praise by the early *Acharya* Manakkal Nambi who is the disciple's disciple of Nadamuni, and the preceptor of Alavandar, the great grandfather of Ramanuja. Ramanuja was just seen as a young man, according to tradition, by Alavandar who had attained to venerable old age then. His preceptor Manakkal Nambi must have been older. There is no reason to doubt the age of Ramanuja, though the actual dates may not, it is just possible, be equally certain. The latter half of the tenth century and the first of the next, at the lowest computation must be the age of Manakkal Nambi. If in his age Kulasekhara's part of the *Prabandha* came in for commendatory verses from him, Kulasekhara must have been somewhat anterior.

CRITICISM OF CERTAIN IDENTIFICATIONS OF THE ALVAR

The identification suggested by the learned doctor is based on the word " Kulasekharanka " which might be interpreted as one possessed of the name Kulasekhara. Kulasekhara is a common enough name for Travancore sovereigns. In fact, in modern times Kulasekhara forms part of the name of every sovereign, and about the time with which we are just at present concerned it is possible to mention two other Kulasekharas with the earlier of whom perhaps this Kulasekharanka may seem, at first sight, to be identical. In the Trivandram Sanskrit series, edited and published from manuscripts, by the learned Pandit Ganapati Sastrigal, there are two works Tapatisamvaranam and Subhadradhananjayam, both of them dramas by a Kulasekharavarma, who is described as ruler of Mahodayapura. He is besides described as "the best of the descendants of the Kerala family." He was a devotee of Vishnu as the final verse of the play expresses a longing for complete devotion to Sridhara. He seems to have been an ardent admirer of the Paramahasmas (ascetics of the highest order). The learned Pundit makes a reference, in the introduction to the first drama, to a contemporary of this prince, the author of the Vyangya Vyakhya. He places the author of this commentary later than the author of the Dasarupaka who flourished in the 10th century A. D. He is also said to be the author of a prose work, Ascharyamanjari, which is quoted in a commentary on the Amarakosa called

Tikasarvasva, in annotating the word *kusala* in the first *Kanda*. In that comment a date is given in Saka and Kaḷi eras corresponding to the year A. D. 1159. From this he ascribes the author to the period between the "latter part of the 10th century and the early part of the 12th century.[1] Mahodayapura the capital of this ruler, is Vanjikulam or Tiruvanjikulam in the modern state of Cochin. It is just possible that this prince is referred to by the name Kulasakharanka in the inscriptions cited by Sir R. G. Bhandarkar ; but it must be noted there is no reference to any war in the dramas under reference, and any identification based on the mere similarity of name will at the very best be only a probable guess which might turn out correct or prove to be wrong. I refer to this ruler here as the learned editor of the Travancore series, identifies him with Kulasekhara Alvar, an identification which we shall presently show to be equally impossible, with the other.

There is another Kulasekhara, this time of Travancore, who in very many particulars might come nearer in point of description and

---

1. Introduction to Tapatisamvaraṇa.

distinctive political achievements to Kulasekhara, Alvar. This was Ravivarman Kulasekhara, sometimes called Ravivarmabhupa merely, the author of the Pradhyumnabhyudaya, and of a commentary on Alankara Sarvasva, the author of which, Samudrabandha by name, states that his work is based on the commentary propounded by Ravivarmadeva at the request of the pundits of his court.[1] We have a number of inscriptions of this ruler and a rather elaborate *prasasti* (panegyric) by a poet Kavibhushana.[2] In addition to being the author of the works above referred to he was a great deal responsible for turning out the Muhammadan garrisons left in the Tamil country after the invasion of Malik Kafur. His inscriptions give the information that he was born in A. D. 1266—7 came to the Keralapadam (Kerala throne) at Kolambapura (Quilon,) in his 33rd year, and got himself anointed victor on the banks of the Vegavati (river running close to Kanchipuram) in his 46th year.[3] He claims conquest as far north as Nellore, and has left behind inscriptions of

1. Introduction to Pradhyumnābhyudaya. p. ii.
2. Epigraphic Indica iv. 149.
3. Epigraphic Indica IV. 146.

s at least as far north as Poonamallee.[1] He aims conquest of the Pandya, Chola and the ongu country, and gives himself the titles *angramadhira* and *Trikshatrachudamani.* If e go by a mere description of achievments, is Ravivarman Kulasekhara[2] would come earest to the Alvar Kulasekhara.

His date however is A. D. 1266 to at least . D. 1316, a date clearly impossible for the lvar for the reasons given in the previous aragraph. There is besides the crucial idence that a record of the Chola Kulottunga's 3th year (A. D. 1088)[3] makes provision for e recital of one of the works of Kulasekhara eginning "Tettarum-tiral". There is an scription[4] in Pagan in Tamil characters of e 13th century according to Dr. E. Hultzrah. his records the construction of a *mantapa,* d the making of provision for burning a lamp the temple by a Kulasekhara Nambi of

1. Epigraphist's Report for 1912.
   Ep. Coll. 34 of 1911.
   Epigraphia Indica VIII. pp. 8 & 9.
2. For the whole of this ruler's history see an article by me in the Eranakulam College Magazine for July 1919.
3. South Indian Inscriptions III. 70 pp. 148-52.
4. Ep. Indica VII. 197-8.

Mahodayarpattinam in *Malaimandalam.* The record begins with quoting stanza 6[1] of the Mukundamala. This quotation and the name of the donor argue priority of the age of, and may justify the assumption even of some antiquity for, the Alvar.

We must look therefore for Kulasekhara, according to the first inscription, at some distance of time before about A. D. 1088. Having regard to the commendatory verses of Manakkal Nambi we shall have to look for him some considerable time anterior to this, and adequately removed from the middle of the 10th century A. D., say from about 950.

KULASEKHARA'S OWN EVIDENCE ON THE POINT

Before passing out of this portion of the subject, let us see what Alvar Kulasekhara has to say of himself in the works of his that have come down to us. Stanza 40 of the Mukundamala gives by way of personal details no more than that the author was king Kula-

---

1. Nāsthā dharmē na vasunichayē naiva kamōpabhōgē
Yadyad bhavyaṁ bhavatu Bhagvan pūrva
[karmānurūpam
Etatprārthyam mama bahumatam janmajamāntarēpi
Tvatpādāmbhōruhayugagatā nischalā bhaktirastu.

sekhara, and he had two friends named Dvijanmavara (best among Brahmans) and Padmasara (one whose arrow was the lotus, a name of the Indian God of Love, Kama). He describes himself otherwise as the devotee of Vishnu which character of his is made clear in every stanza of the Sanskrit work. The part of his work included in the Tamil *Prabandham* comprises 105 stanzas, and goes by the collective name of *Perumal Tirumoli* the first word having reference to the latter part of his name Kulasekhara Perumal. In the last stanza of every section of 10 he describes himself as the author and gives some personal details. Taking them all together these facts in regard to him stand out: his name was Kulasekhara, he was ruler of Kolli (Quilon); he was master of Kudal (Madura); he was ruler over Koli (Uraiyur, the Chola Capital). In another of these stanzas he calls himself the ruler over Kongu.[1] Thus then we have a ruler whose patrimony was the kingdom of Travancore, with its capital Quilon. Sometime in the course of his career he became entitled either to the rule or overlordship of the Pandya and the Chola kingdoms with their capitals

1. Perumāl Tirumoḷi, I. 10, II. 10, III. 10 in particular

respectively of Madura and Uraiyur. He seems also to have acquired possession of Kongu. Thus he would have become ruler over the whole of the possession of Ravivarman Kulasekhara referred to above. The inscription of date A. D. 1088, and the commendatory verses of Manakkal Nambi make the identification of Ravivarman Kulasekhara with the Alvar impossible. Alvar Kulasekhara has therefore to be located at a period of time anterior to Manakkal Nambi. The ascendancy of Travancore which these achievements of Kulasekhara implies, does not at all seem possible after A. D. 900 when the first great Chola Parantaka became supreme in South India when the Chola Capital was Tanjore, not Uraiyur. We are therefore bound to look for his position sometime earlier than 900. If his ascendancy was a historical fact since we have it in so many words from himself alone, we shall have to put his time of life at some period when the disposition of powers in South India would admit of a Kerala overlordship. Such ascendancy would have been possible either before the rise of the great Pallavas under the dynasty of Narasimhavarman sometime before A. D. 600, or after the collapse of this dynasty following the death of the great Pallava Nandivarman, which probably took place sometime about A. D. 800. If Tirumangai Alvar is really the last Alvar, and if we are bound to find a place for Kulasekhara before him, Kulasekhara may have to be given a place anterior to the rise of the great Pallavas sometime in the sixth century A. D. The specific reference[1] of Tirumangai Alvar to the occupation of Kanchi by an overlord of the Pallava, by name Vairamega, the first Rastrakuta Dantidurga, makes Tirumangai Alvar's position as certain as we can possibly get to. This leads us to the question of the chronological order of the Alvars.

THE CHRONOLOGICAL ORDER OF THE ALVARS

Coming to the question of a recognised order we have already indicated that the Ramanuja Nurrandadi of Amudan of Arangam leads to the inference of a recognised chronological order.

---

1. மன்னவன் றொண்டையர் கோன்வணங்கும் நீண்முடிமாலை [வயிரமேகன்
தன்வலிதன் புகழ்சூழ்ந்த கச்சியட்ட புயகரத்தாதிதன்னை
கன்னிநன் மாமதில் மங்கை வேந்தன் காமருசீர்க் [கலிகன்றிகுன்றா
வின்னிசையால் சொன்ன செஞ்சொல் மாலையேத்த [வல்லார்க்கிடம் வைகுந்தமே.

Periya Tirumoḻi, II. 8, 10.

One of the two elements of difference in the order was explained leaving only one item, that is, the position of Tiruppan Alvar about whom there is a difference among the authorities. The list that was set out at the commencement from Sir R. G. Bhandarkar's book is the order of precedence according to the fabulously fanciful dates given to these Alvars. When hagiologists actually attempted to give these precise dates, the order seems to have been a recognised fact. Vedanta Desika has a section of his *Prabandham*, the 19th in order, which he calls *Prabandha Saram* of 18 stanzas. The first stanza is by way of introduction ; the next 12 are devoted one stanza each to the Alvars, and they are set out in the following order giving the name of the Alvar and alluding to the actual works, and the number of stanzas contained therein, of each of the Alvars.

Poygai Alvar,
Bhudat Alvar,
Pey Alvar,
Tirumalisai Alvar,
Nam Alvar,
Madhurakavi,
Kulasekhara,

Periya Alvar,
Andal,
Tondaradippodi,
Tiruppanalvar,
Tirumangai Alvar.

Stanza 14 deals similarly with the Ramanuja Nurrandadi of Amudan of Arangam making up the *Prabandham* 4000. Stanzas 15 and 16 repeat the counting of the stanzas, and stanza 17 gives the names in the order in which they were before recounted. The last stanza is the usual *Phalasruti* giving the name of the author of the work *Prabandhasaram.* It cannot be said that Vedanta Desika in thus composing the *Prabandhasaram* did not know the *Ramanuja Nurrandadi*, or the differences in the order in which Tiruppan Alvar and Nam Alvar happened to be mentioned there. Either he regarded the order followed by Amudan of Arangam not chronological, or because he knew that these differences in the said author were, at any rate in his opinion, due to error. In any case we are bound to accept the order of precedence set out by Vedanta Desika as the authoritative order in his time. But the chief question in connection with this order is whether it was meant to be chronological. The probabilities are that they were, and the most that can be said against Vedanta Desika's order being chronological is that it was the order of precedence in point of time set out by hagiologists who came before him. As a matter of fact in the form in which the *guruparamparas* have come down to us the most elaborate among them are the works of a disciple and disciple's disciple of Vedanta Desika. Their works were based on the previously existing *guruparamparas* of which one at least went back to the time of Ramanuja. Therefore then the order in which the names of these Alvars are arranged seem the chronological order, at any rate the chronological order conceived by those as long back from us as Ramanuja himself. We can hardly infer more from this order as stanza 8 referring to Kulasekhara states that the Alvar was born in Vanjikulam.[1] The Alvar himself states that he

---

1. Stanza 8, Prabandhasāram.

பொன்புரையும் வேற்குலசேகரனை மாசிப்புனர்பூசத் தெழில்
வஞ்சிக் களத்திற்றோன்றி

அன்புடனே நம்பெருமான் செம்பொற் கோயிலனைத்துலகின்
பெருவாழ்வு மடியார் தங்கள்

was ruler of Kolli (Quilon). It is just possible he was the son of the ruler of Travancore, but was born actually in Tiruvanjikkalam. It would not be constructive criticism not to recognise this order except for very satisfactorily substantial reasons. Such have not been advanced in regard to Kulasekhara as we have pointed out above. An attempt has been made to bring Nam Alvar chronologically to the position of the last of them all, which goes against the grain of Vaishnava tradition, and for which the positive proofs offered are perhaps not worth criticism, in the way that they are offered. There are points in them which it will be just as well we examine here.

இன்பமிகு பெருங்குழு உக்காணமன் மேலிருளிரிய வென்றெ
டுத்த விசையிற் சொன்ன
நன்பொருள்சேர் திருமொழி நூற்றைந்து பாட்டு நன்குரக வென
க்கருள்செய் நல்விதியே.

See also extract from the Bhāgavatam quoted above referring specifically to Periyār-note. 1, p. 8.

LECTURE III.

WAS NAM ALVAR THE LAST OF THEM ALL ?

Nam Alvar whose "baptismal" name was Maran son of Kari is by pre-eminence known by the name Nam Alvar meaning 'our Alvar' said by the hagiologists to have been given to him by no less an authority than Lord Ranganatha at Srirangam. It was already pointed out that he is regarded as having followed the first four Alvars, and as a consequence, among those of them whose life was cast in a period of considerable antiquity.

GURUPARAMPARAI ACCOUNT

According to the guruparamparai account Nam Alvar was born on the 43rd day of Kali, the year Pramadi on the full moon of the month of Vaisakha, Friday, Visakha. He was born at Kurukai, the son of the adhikari of the township by name Kari and his wife Udayanangai. From birth the baby conducted itself peculiarly taking no nourishment, nor doing what children do in that stage. The parents in sorrow for this peculiar birth gave him the name Maran and set him in front of the god and goddess of the Vishnu temple in the locality The child is said to have crawled along to the front of the temple where there was a tamarind tree and assumed his seat at the foot of the tree in what is called *Yogamudra* (the attitude of one rapt in deep contemplation). He is supposed to have continued in this state for 16 years when he obtained the inspiration by favour of Vishnu which found vent ultimately in the part of the *Prabandham* ascribed to him.

Such as he was he required some one to propagate his gospel. The fit instrument for this purpose appeared in the person of a Brahman of the " top-knot " community of the Samavedi section in the village Tirukkolur in the Tinnevelly district. He is, according to this account, said to have been born in the "*Dvapara yuga*" 863, 879th year, the year Isvara, month Chittirai, the 14th of the bright fortnight, Friday, nakshatra Chitra. Having done his schooling he went on a pilgrimage, and while in the north in Ayodhya, he turned towards his native place one night, and while casting his eyes in that direction he is said to have sighted a great column of light of an unusual character. Being curious to know what it was, he thought of returning to his native country and kept journeying along in the direction of the light. At last he came to Alvar Tirunagari or Kurukai, wherefrom he took the direction towards the south. As soon as he moved out towards the south he found the light changing position to the north. He returned to the locality where the light appeared to him and searching for what might be the cause he discovered the presence of the miraculous Alvar indicated. He remained there for some time and putting Nam Alvar a particularly recondite question he got an answer that satisfied him. He therefore sat down to receive the inspiration of the Alvar which would throw light upon the various problems of life and religion, which agitated him. Nam Alvar gave his exposition at the instance of Vishnu himself in the works included in the *Prabandham*. They are supposed to embody the truths that lay hidden in the four Vedas [1] and thus provided the means for the attain-

---

1. கண்டுகொண்டென்னைக் காரிமாறப்பிரான்
பண்டைவல் வினைபாற்றியருளினான்
எண்டிசையு மறிய வியம்புகேன்
ஒண்டமிழ்ச் சடகோப னருளையே. (7)

ment of salvation even to those who could not either read or understand the esoteric learning of the Vedanta. Madhurakavi is stated to have committed to writing what fell by word of mouth from Nam Alvar. When Nam Alvar passed away in his 35th year Madhurakavi immediately set up an idol of the Alvar and was believed to have been worshipping this idol for 50 years after, continuing the teaching of the 4 *Prabandhams* of Nam Alvar, viz. Tiruviruttam, Tiruvasiriyam, Periya Tiruvandadi and Tiruvaymoli. Madhurakavi's special contribution was the discovery of a spiritual preceptor (Acharya) and the need of such a preceptor is, what he gives expression to, as his peculiar teaching in the 11 verses of his included in the *Prabandham* literature. Among those that contributed commendatory verses to

---

அருள் கொண்டாடுமடியவரின்புற
அருளினா னவ்வருமறையின் பொருள்
அருள்கொண்டாயிர மின்றமிழ்பாடினான்
அருள் கண்டீரிவ்வுலகினில் மிக்கதே (8)

மிக்கவேதியர் வேதத்தினுட்பொருள்
நிற்கப்பாடி யென் னெஞ்சுள் நிறுத்தினான்
தக்கசீர்ச் சடகோபனென்னம்பிக்காட்
புக்க காதலடிமைப் பயனன்றே. (9)

Madhurakavi in the Prabandham.

the works of Nam Alvar are Nathamuni, his grandson Alavandar and the spiritual successor of Ramanuja, Pillan, not to mention the one stanza ascribed to Madhurakavi himself. Madhurakavi himself received two verses of commendation from Nathamuni. This is so far the traditional account preserved in the guruparamparas. We shall proceed to an examination of this.

As against this tradition one effort has been made at an identification by the Epigraphists. A certain minister of an early Pandya king is given the name Maran Kari, and is described as a "madhurakavi." Minister Madhurakavi was somehow equated with this Alvar and was made therefore posterior to this particular inscription of A. D. 770.[1] The main reason for this is that Nam Alvar is traditionally said to have had a disciple by name Madhurakavi whose 11 stanzas upon his attainment of the proper "*Guru*" in Nam Alvar is included in the "*Prabandham.*" Other details of the life of this Nam Alvar and his disciple as recorded in living tradition go against this identification, and at the very best the identification on the

1. The Anaimalai Ins. Ep. Ind. VIII p. 317—321.

basis of the occurrence of the descriptive epithet "madhurakavi" to the neglect of all the other essential details is of doubtful validity. It is on a par with the inference that Kulasekhara was later than Ramanuja because the Mukundamala contains the word Ramanuja.

There has however been a more pretentious effort to make him the last of the Alvars by the author of the "Tamil Studies" which while it exhibits a considerable amount of learning bases its argument throughout upon assumptions of the most unwarranted character. Passing over what are perhaps positive misrepresentations of others, it is not desirable here even to go into the whole of the details; but the main arguments deserve to be examined. The first assumption of this author warranted by no historical source is that Nathamuni was a personal disciple of Nam Alvar: "he had two disciples—Sri Nadamuni and Madhurakavi—to whom he taught his Tiruvaymoli and *other Prabandhams.*" Even according to him the first heads the list of the "Acharayas" while the second is elevated to the rank of a saint (Alvar). In regard to the fact that Nathamuni was a disciple of Nam Alvar no reason whatsoever is given nor any source of the information indicated. Tradition merely states Nathamuni drew, by *yogic* practice, the forgotten Tiruvaymoli from Nam Alvar with the assistance of "a disciple" of Madhurakavi. If tradition is accepted it ought to be properly interpreted and explained; otherwise it ought to be given up. There is no evidence given for this assumption of discipleship on the part of the first Acharya. If the two were alike disciples why is the one only an Acharya and why is the other an Alvar. This differential treatment requires some explanation; none such is offered. The Alvar belongs to the earlier group and the Acharya to the later according to accepted Vaishnava tradition.

In regard to this matter he has further dow some arguments drawn from a misrepresentation, at the very best misunderstanding, of a statement of mine, in my article on Tirumangai Alvar, in the Indian Antiquary for 1906. We shall return to this later.

The first argument in favour of the position of Nam Alvar as the last of the Alvars is the crucial argument, according to this author, of philology. He mentions a certain number of Sanskrit words which are used by the Alvar and which he says do not occur in the Sangam works. I will take just two out of a list that he gives. He speaks of Sodi (Sans. Jyotis) and Makavaikundam (Sans. Magha or Makha-Vaikuntha). The first word is found in the Tiruvasakam of Manikkavasagar and, Tevaram of Appar and part at least of second term occurs in the very early Sangam works Paripadal and Purananuru. He refers again to two gramatical forms, the use of a double plural form, and the use of a particular tense particle, which is stated to be the usage of "this time" by the commentator Nachchinarkiniyar. The commentator apparently uses the expression " this time " to mean the time following the classical age and does not seem to imply any very narrow limits. The crucial test according to this author would thus fail.

The second argument is based upon the fact that the works of the Alvars give evidence of following the age of the Puranas, and he refers to a passage of Nam Alvar where there is an apparent reference to the Lingapurana.[1] This

---

1. இலிங்கத்திட்ட புராணத்தீரும் சமணரும் சாக்கியரும்
வலிந்துவாது செய்வீர்களும் மற்றுநுந்தெய்வமுமாகிநின்றான்
மலிந்து செந்நெல் கவரிவீசும் திருக்குருகூரதனுள்
பொலிந்து நின்ற பிரான்கண்டீர்ஒன்றும் பொய்யில்லைபோற்
IV. 10. 5.] றுமினே.

begs the question. The age of the Puranas cannot yet be regarded as such a settled matter to admit of decisive applications in this fashion. We shall have to revert to it again. Another part of this argument, is a reference in Nam Alvar to the use of flowers, incense, lamps, unguents and water in the process of worship.[1] He says that these are from the rules laid down in the Puranas. It will perhaps be more accurate to say these are the forms of worship according to the Agamas, at any rate, the Pancharatra Agama.

The next is an argument based upon the statement that " the chewing of betel-leaves was almost unknown to the Hindu populace prior to A. D. 500 ". The mention of the word betel by the Alvar is held to involve the " chewing of betel-leaves by the populace ". A quotation is made from the Silappadhikaram, which this scholar describes as belonging to the second century A. D., where there is a clear

---

1. மேவித்தொழுதுய் மினீர்கள்வேதப் புனிதவிருக்கை
நாவிற்கொண்டச் சுதன்றன்னை ஞானவிதி பிழையாமே
பூவில் புகையும் விளக்கும் சாந்தமும் நீரும் மலிந்து
மேவித் தொழு மடியாரும் பகவரும் மிக்க துலகே.

V. 2. 9.

reference to the chewing of betel-leaves; but he gets round this inconvenience with the remark " but we doubt whether the custom had been so universal in the days of Ilango-Adikal, as it was in our Alvar's time. " The assumption in the first part of this remark as well as that in the next requires some demonstration.[1]

The next argument is based upon the absence of any acrimonious reference in Nam Alvar's works to the Saiva sect which he finds in some considerable number in the works of the other Alvars such as Tirumalisai, Tirumangai and Tondaradippodi, etc. He draws the inference therefrom that this conciliatory attitude of Nam Alvar towards the

1. உண்ணுஞ்-சோறும் பருகுநீர் தின்னும் வெற்றிலையு மெல்லாம்
கண்ணனெம் பெருமானென்றென்றே கண்கள் நீர் மல்கி
மண்ணினுளவன் சீர்வளம் மிக்க வனூர் வினவி
திண்ணமென்னிளமான் புகுமூர் திருக்கோளூரே.

Tiruvāymoḷi VI. VII. 1.

உண்டினி திருந்தவுயர் பேராளர்க்
கம்மென் றிரைய லோடடைக்காயீத்த
மையீரோதியை வருகெனப் பொருந்தி.

Śilappadhikāram. XVI. ll. 54-56. p. 384.

பாசவர்—இலையமுதிடுவார்.
வெற்றிலைக்கட்டுவோர் (அரும்பதவுரை.)

Referring to betel leaf and nuts bazar

Ibid. V. 26.

Saivas was due to "a sort of reconciliation (that) had been effected among the Saivas and Vaishnavas", after Jainism and Buddhism had been vanquished. Having regard to the age that this scholar has ascribed to Nam Alvar it would he hardly possible to believe, from what we know of the history of the period, that such reconciliation had beenn effected at all. The normal inference from this conciliatory spirit would be that Nam Alvar lived at a time when Vaishnavism and Saivism had to organise themselves as against Buddhism and Jainism, rather than to a later period when a historically unwarranted reconciliation has to be postulated.

The next argument involves two assumptions; the first is that if according to tradition Tirumangai Alvar made arrangements for the recital of the *Tiruvaymoli* annually in Srirangam the author of the *Tiruvaymoli* must have visited Srirangam. How the one follows from the other it is not clear to see. Supposing as tradition says Tirumangai Alvar did much for organising worship at Srirangam and supposing that he felt drawn to the *Tiruvaymoli* of Nam Alvar which he arranged should be recited at a particular period of the year in Srirangam, how does that affect Nam Alvar one way or the other? If the supposition of the Tirumangai Alvar's doing be accepted as fact, the author of the *Tiruvaymoli* must have been an anterior personage who would not be affected by the consideration either way. Nam Alvar might have visited Srirangam or might not have. It does not appear he did from what we know of his works. It is hardly necessary that a temple should be visited in order to celebrate it in a set of verses. The contrary assumption is one that the author has fallen into and we may have to refer to it in another connection.

The next assumption here is that because a place by name Varagunamangai is referred to in one of the poems of Nam Alvar, he must be posterior to Varaguna Pandya from whose name it is assumed Varagunamangai took its name. We know from inscriptional records only of two Varagunas so far; it is just possible there were more who did not hand down their names to us in inscriptions; but where is the necessity that a temple Varagunamangai should inevitably draw its name from Varaguna Pandya? We do know of numbers of instances in which names are so given, but that does not follow logically that the obverse statement that wherever there is such a name it must always have been drawn from a particular person. This scholar has made an application of this kind, in connection with Tirumalisai Alvar, where there is a reference to a Gunabhara which is interpreted as referring to the Pallava Mahendra Varman I.[1] The passage there refers to the Gunabhara who 'gave us our body and protects us in it' and continues that 'those that have learnt the truth will never find the courage to give Him up'. How a reference to an earthly ruler can be read into this term Gunabhara so used, ordinary human intelligence fails to understand. If it were a term used in connection with a particular temple or with a particular form of god in a temple which might otherwise be connected with the Pallavas, one may see a subtle reference to the living ruler as a compliment. This is a supremely good illustration of where such applications fail. Nam Alvar's reference to Vara-

---

1. Stanza 93 of the Nānmukhan Tiru Andādi.

காப்பு மறந்தறியேன் கண்ணனே யென்றிருப்பன்
ஆப்பங் கொழிய வும்பல்லுயிர்க்கும்—ஆக்கை
கொடுத்தளித்த கோனே குணப்பரனே உன்னை
விடத்துணியார் மெய்தெளிந்தார் தாம்.

gunamangai is of almost the same character. Both terms are terms of common use among the Vaishnavas; because a *bhakta* has to postulate the "Saguna Brahmam" as opposed to the "Nirguna One", and gunas (qualities) ascribed to such a Being cannot be the ordinary gunas. That is the import of these expressions, and unless reference to a human sovereign is otherwise actually warranted it will not do to put that interpretation upon them.

The next argument is that Nam Alvar omits the celebration of Srivilliputtur, as also Tirumangai. This omission is explained in the case of the latter as due to the non-existence of the temple in this place, and in the case of the former to the fact that though it had come into existence it was not sufficiently prominent. The futility of such an argument is apparent in the obvious *petitio principi*.

The next argument is that the *Tiruvaymoli* hymns are set to particular tunes while those of even Tirumangai Alvar are not. This is ascribed to the Vaishnavas having copied this arrangement from the 'Saivas who adopted it invariably, and since this arrangement' is preserved only for Nam Alvar he must have been later. Even in respect of the Saiva Adiyars this was an arrangement introduced not by the authors themselves but by others. It requires musicians to do it. The ancient classic "Parripadal" gives at the end of each poem the name of the author and the name of the person who set it to tune distinctly. That apparently refers to the custom that it was the musician, or the professional class of people whose duty it was to sing these, to set these poems to tunes. Whether the Saivas copied the Vaishnavas or the Vaishnavas copied the Saivas, or both of them copied from something older, or each of them followed the established custom, this arrangement is no particular test of age.

The next argument has reference to that of the Epigraphists already referred to at the outset and he falls foul of them because their argument would lead to the conclusion that Nam Alvar lived prior to A. D. 770. Because Nam Alvar has not celebrated the deity in the temple at Anai Malai which was founded in the year A. D. 770, the inference is drawn that "the Alvar must therefore have lived either before or long after A.D. 770; but the impossibility of the first has been proved in previous pages." He postulates the hypothesis the village built at so much expenditure in A. D. 770 had fallen into ruins by A. D. 900, and hence Nam Alvar could not refer to it.

" The last, the most important argument in favour of our theory that Satagopan was the last of all the Vaishnava Saints is furnished by the age of Nathamuni, *one of his two esteemed disciples.*" It is here that a misrepresentation of my statement comes in. According to the traditional statement, Nathamuni is said to have been born in A. D. 582, and after remaining in " *Samadhi* " at the foot of Nam Alvar's tamarind tree for over 300 years he died in A. D. 922. I wrote, discussing just exactly the points in the life of Nathamuni that this scholar takes into consideration, that " it certainly would not be unreasonable to ascribe Nathamuni to a period beginning with the earlier half of the 10th century A. D. This is exactly the conclusion warranted by the proper understanding of the traditional account, which is that Nathamuni was born in A. D. 582 and that he was in what is called " Yogasamadhi " for 340 years. This would give the date A. D. 922 for the death of Nathamuni, which is not at all improbable, taking all circumstances into consideration. Why did the hagiologists then ascribe this long life or long death in life to Nathamuni ? The explanation is not far to seek. They believed and the Vaishnavas do believe even now, that there was an unbroken succession of these saints, and unfortunately they found a gap between Nathamuni and the last Alvar. This they bridged over in this clumsy fashion." On the basis of this I am convicted with believing in the statement that Nathamuni was born in 582. Let that pass. We have already pointed out that there is no reason whatsoever to assume that Nathamuni was a disciple of Nam Alvar except in a metaphorical sense. Coming to the actual facts, Nathamuni's age is sought to be determined by his having been born in a village Vira Narayanapuram taken to be a foundation of the Chola king Vira Narayana or Parantaka I ; by his having died in Gangaigondasolapuram, the foundation of Rajendra, the Gangaigondasola, A. D. 1011-1042 ; and by the fact that he was the grandfather of Alavandar who died at Srirangam when Ramanuja was a young man. In regard to part I, who is it that ascribes the birth of the Acharya to Vira Narayanapuram ? His biographer, whoever he was, and at the time of the biographer the place was known as Vira Narayanapuram. The Cholas were in the habit of changing the names of places in this fashion, and it does not mean that the place was not in existence before, nor the temple in it. It is to-day known by the name Kurukaikkavalappan Kovil. It must have been known perhaps by that name before, and Nathamuni could have been born in the village without coming after Parantaka. He died at Gangaigondasolapuram. That again was not altogether a new foundation. It is hardly a mile and a half from the first place, the place of birth ; it is just possible there was a village there anterior to the springing up of the Capital city. There are numbers of respectable villages about. There is nothing to prevent Nathamuni having died in one of these places which the later biographer refers to by the name of the vast capital city which took in all the villages around within its own limits. The traditional account, however, says that he returned to his village to die. The last fact is that Alavandar, the grandson of Nathamuni, died very old when Ramanuja was just a young man, may be about 25. That is the fact upon which we have to go. Whatever be the value of the horoscopes, or the actual dates of Ramanuja, as given in the *guruparampara* there can be no doubt about the period of his life which was the later half of the 11th century A. D. and the first part of the following century. Alavandar might have been born about 60 years before him, and Nathamuni his grandfather about that length or a little more; so that a difference of 120 to 150 years between Nathamuni and Ramanuja would not err on the side of too much liberality. That would mean Nathamuni was born somewhere about A. D. 900. But that is of no use to this question as the direct discipleship of Nathamuni to Nam Alvar is a mere unwarranted assumption. If an inference could be drawn from traditions preserved by *hagiologists*, we ought to look for Nam Alvar the three centuries and a half almost of the *yogic* years of Nathamuni previous to the age of the latter. That would take us to the middle of the sixth century, in itself perhaps not an improbable time. We shall investigate this further later on in the course of this thesis.

Before passing on it would be just as well to point out that it is not in any spirit of carping that this somewhat detailed criticism of other views is offered. This investigation of other views has no further object than a critical re-valuation of the arguments for the purposc of acceptance or rejection. We hope that this long investigation upon the position of Nam Alvar as the latest of the group proves that the contention is, on the basis of the facts adducad, untenable.

THE GENERAL POSITION OF THE ALVARS

Coming to the general position of these Alvars we have already noted the opinion of the learned doctor that they must have flourished about the time of the revival of Brahmanism and Hinduism in the north about the 5th or the 6th century A. D. He admits the possibility that Vaishnavism might have penetrated to the south as early as about the first century A. D. In the group of the twelve Alvars, the Vaishnavas regard the three names, in the order as in the list set forth at the beginning of this thesis, as the first: not the first in eminence as undoubtedly that position of eminence is given to Nam Alvar. The first therefore in Tamil, which may be priority in rank or in time alike, must refer to priority in point of time in this particular context. The fourth name in the list is traditionally also brought in along with this group of three, but that tradition however exhibits the clumsy efforts by means of which this position is sought to be attained. According to the story Bhaktisara or Tirumalisai had to remain for the long period of 700 years in the "*Yogasamadhi*" to come into contact with a Pallava ruler of Kanchi. This is apparently the usual clumsy effort to get over the chronological incompatibility when the hagiologists set about attempting a precise chronology; but the association between Bhaktisara with the shrine Yadhoktakari preserved in the tradition is, in all probability true. There are a few separate verses quoted to support his connection with the locality, and what transpired there between him and the Pallava king of the town; being fugitive pieces they are open to the suspicion that they might have been composed for the purpose by others, but there is one unlooked for piece of evidence which seems to lend some support to the association of Bhaktisara with this particular shrine in Kanchi on the one side and a Pallava ruler on the other. A long poem of the Sangam collection called Pattuppattu refers itself to the early ruler of Kanchi known to literature as Tondaman Ilandirayan, describing him as a patron whose bounty would satisfy the utmost wishes of those that sought it. The poet leads on his prospective bard seeking patronage through various localities outside Kanchi, and entering within makes specific reference only to this shrine of Yadhoktakari called in Tamil Vehka.[1] The author of this poem was a Brahman described as Kadiyalur Rudran Kannanar who also celebrates in another poem of the same collection the great ancient Chola Karikala. This raises the presumption that the Pallava contemporary of Bhaktisara was probably the Tondaman Ilandirayan.

Tondaman Ilandirayan turns out from a reference to him by Poygai Alvar to have been contemporaneous with him, and in a way confirms the presumption raised by the indirect reference in Bhaktisara. The Vehka or Yadoktakari, referred to above as specially connected with Bhaktisara, "the God doing his bidding" as the Sanskrit name means, was the birthplace of Poygai Alvar whatever his particular

1. நீடுகுலைக் காந்தளஞ் சிலம்பிற் களிறுபடிந்தாங்குப்
பாம்பணைப்பள்ளியமர்ந் தோனாங்கண்.

Perumbāṇaṟṟuppāḍai ll. 371-3.

age. Before investigating the evidence available to locate Poygai Alvar, it would be necessary to consider the period allotted to him in the work already drawn upon in connection with Nam Alvar. This work quotes a stanza each from Poygai Alvar and Pey Alvar, [1] which refer to a place called Vinnagaram where God Vishnu is said to have been seated while in three other holy shrines mentioned along with this in the same stanza he is stated respectively to be standing, lying and walking. The place mentioned in the order of standing, sitting, lying and walking are Venkadam (Tirupati), Vinnagar, Vehka (Yadhoktakari) at Kanchi and Tirukkovalur. The philologists author would derive the Tamil Vinnagar from Vishnu-Nagar which has no justification in grammar for the kind of coalescence brought

---

1. First Andādi 77.
வேங்கடமும் விண்ணகரும் வெஃகாவுமஃகாத
பூங்கிடங்கினீள் கோவல் பொன்னகரும்—நான்கிட
த்தும்
நின்றானிருந்தான் கிடந்தான் நடந்தானே
என்றால் கெடுமாமிடர்.

Third Andādi. 62.
விண்ணகரம் வெஃகாவிரிதிரை நீர் வேங்கடம்
மண்ணகரம் மாமாட வேளுக்கை—மண்ணகத்த
தென்குடந்தை தேனார் திருவரங்கம் தென்கோட்டி
தன் குடங்கை நீரேற்றான் தாழ்வு.

about by the combination of the words. Dr. Hultzsch and his assistants derived it from *Vishnu Griha.* It will be seen in the second of the stanzas referred to above that it is brought in contrast with Man-nagar (city on earth). This compound is Vin-nagar (city of Heaven). That is again another matter. Deriving it in this manner, he seeks to identify the place with Paramesvara Vinnagar of Tirumangai Alvar, taken by Dr. Hultzsch* to have been built by the Pallava king Paramesvara Varman. This identification is made on the ground that the other places mentioned in connection with this Vin-nagar are in Tondai Nadu (Pallava country), and that Poygai and Pey Alvar were "local saints and their peregrinations were confined to Tondai Nadu ". The other places are not all of them in Tondai Nadu, and if Tirukkottiyur and Tirumalirunjolai are well known, so are Tiruvengadam and Tirukkovalur. The wrong notion arises in the conception that every place referred to by an Alvar must have been visited by him. The absurdity of the position becomes apparent when the second of these Alvars referred to Parkkadal (Kshirabdi) and Vaikuntham itself to either of which certainly he did not travel in the course of his peregrinations. These are mere allusions to places of holy reputation at the time. The case is different when an Alvar lays himself out to celebrate a particular shrine when the presumption of a visit and actual presence may be warranted. It is unnecessary to postulate a visit and absurdly narrow the area of the peregrinations of these saints. Coming to the Vinnagar under discussion there are five of these in the Chola country in addition to Paramesvara Vinnagaram in Kanchi. The actual reference here is Vaikuntha Vinnagar near Shiyali in the Tanjore district. The only difficulty about this identification is that it does not enable us to bring the Alvars down to a period of our own choice, the latter half of the seventh century A. D.

LECTURE IV

THE FIRST ALVARS

Let us now proceed on the way that the evidence leads us—Poygai, Bhutam, Pey, are all three of them regarded the first Alvars in point of time. With them Tirumalisai gets associated later. This last is closely associated with Vehka (Yadhoktakari temple) in Kanchi by a miracle that Vishnu performed by vacating the temple first and returning to it afterwards, at the bidding of his devotee. The shrine is mentioned as a prominent feature of Kanchi in the poem Perumbanarruppadai of Rudran Kannanar. The commentary on the work on Tamil prosody called Yapparungalam quotes largely from one author, who is referred to as Poygaiyar. Of these quotations two verses[1] are much to the point here.

---

1. ஆழியிழைப்பப் பகல்போ மிராவரிற்
றோழிதுணையாத்துயர் தீரும்.—வாழி
நறுமாலைத் தாராய்த் நிறையயவோ தேவென்னுஞ்
சிறுமாலை சென்றடையும்போது. [pp. 45 and 518.

அவிழ்ந்த துணி யசைக்கு மம்பலமுஞ் சீக்கும்
மகிழ்ந்திடுவார் முன்னமலரும்—கவிழ்ந்து
கிழமுழையாளை நெடுமாக் கிள்ளி
கழுமொழாமன்னவர் தங்கை. [p. 133.

Dewan Bahadur S. Bhavanandam Pillai's edition of Yāpparungala Vrittiyurai. Messrs Longmans & Co.

The first of these specifies the name of Tirayan, and the second a Chola ruler Terk-killi. The commentary refers to the first as the "natural name". Poygaiyar speaking of the Chola and Pallava in compliment together would make all three, the author and the two patrons, contemporary. It must be remembered in this connection that the character of the reference leaves something to be desired. The larger section of Tamil grammar dealing "with import" (Artha of Sans, and "poruḷ" of Tamil) has its first two sections devoted respectively to "emotion" and "action". It is a recognised convention that the treatment of a subject in the first mode is of the "dramatic character" (nadaha valakku); and that in the second mode is of the character of "actual life" (ulagavalakku[1].) These two references are of the former category; but there is no point in the reference, unless it was made as a compliment either to the patron himself or to a descendent of his. Hence these references may be interpreted as meant in direct address

---

1. See. Iḻam—Pūraṇar's Comment on Sūtra 56 of Ahapporuḷ.

(Mr. V. O. Ghidambaram Pillai's edition)

to the patron concerned. The mention of Tirayan and Terkkilli by a single author makes the former Ilam Tirayan, as the latter is among the Chola sovereigns who succeeded the great Chola Karikala on the Chola throne.

Among the Chola sovereigns that figure in Purananuru one name occurs prominently, and that is the name of the Chola Nalam Killi. He is otherwise known Set Chenni, Putpahai and Tervankilli.[1] He had a brother by name Mavalattan. He won a victory against the Pandyas and took seven of their forts,[2] hoisting his own flag on them. He went to war against his own cousins and laid siege to Avur and Uraiyur.[3] Among his enemies figures one of his own cousins Nedum Killi

---

1. Puram 43. 9-11.

   நேரார்க்கடந்த முரண்மிகு திருவிற்
   றேர்வண் கிள்ளி தம்பி வார்கோற்
   கொடுமா மறவர் பெரும.

2. Puram 33. 7-9.

   தென்னன் பொருப்ப நன்னாட்டுள்ளும்
   ஏழெயிற் கதவமெறிந்து கைக்கொண்டுநின்
   பேழ்வாயுழுவை பொறிக்கு மாற்றலை.

3. Ibid. 44 & 45.

who is otherwise known Kariyarruttunjiya Nedum Killi. There are good reasons for regarding this latter as the Chola who succeeded the great Karikala.[1]

There are seventeen poems celebrating this Nalam Killi in the collection Purananuru. The other personage referred to, Tirayan, is known to the literature of this period only as Ilandirayan associated closely with Kanchi as its viceroy. Thus these two rulers come in the generation following almost immediately that of the great Chola Karikala.

From what was said we come to the conclusion that there was a Poygaiyar who was contemporary, in all probability, with the Tondaman Ilam Tirayan and the Chola Nalam Killi. This author is quoted in the commentary on Yapparungalum as Poygaiyar. There are other quotations from Poygaiyar, in this commentary and in that of Perasiriyar (equivalent of the Sans. Mahacharya) on the old grammatical work Tolkappiyam, which gives a few details in regard to the author. Perasiriyar who is a much older commentator than the other, and is among commentators one of the most

1. Ancient India. pp. 352-55.

respected refers to the "andadi" verses of Poygaiyar[1] and *others*, and puts these alongside of the old classical work Muttollayiram. This is an unmistakable indication that the Poygaiyar quoted is the Alvar, as his main work, and the only one in the Tamil Prabandham, is the first Tiruvandadi. The purpose of the quotation in this particular connection is to illustrate that other and abnormal modes of composing verses than those laid down for the particular class were already in considerable vogue. This idea of independence of the rules of prosody in authors is noted in regard to Poygaiyar by the other commentator in his comment on Sutra 40. After quoting three stanzas of Poygaiyar's, irregular from the strict grammatical point of view, the commentator proceeds to note that, though these are irregular they ought to be accepted as "arsha" (Tam aridam). He defines "arsham" as the composition of "rishis" who were able to understand all about "this life, "the life here-

1. Comment on Sūtra 240 of the section on Prosody p. 552 of the late Mr. C. W. Thamotharam Pillai's edition under the mistaken name Nachchinārkiniyar's commentary.

after " and the past, present and future, quoting as his authority the old work on prosody called *Pattiyalmarabu*. Hence it is clear that in comparatively early times even, Poygaiyar came to be regarded as a "superhuman" personality. In commenting on Sutra 94, this same commentator quotes two stanzas[1] of the first Tiruvandadi of Poygai-Alvar under the name Poygaiyar as in the other cases before. This quotation puts it beyond doubt that the Poygaiyar of the commentator is no other than Poygai Alvar. It is clear from this series of references that the poet Poygaiyar quoted as authority is the Alvar, and that he apparently was the author of other works than the one appearing under his name in the *Prabandham* collection. There is one such recently published which exhibits the characteristic features of this Alvar's composition, besides giving conclusive evidence of the author's devotion to Vishnu. This is the work called "*Innilai*" included in the Sangam collection of "shorter poems". This work of 45 stanzas challenges ready comparison with the Kural, and is deservedly held in high esteem. It shows the

---

1. 51 and 69 of the first Tiruvandādi.

peculiarities of versification and archaisms in language that would stamp it as the work of the Alvar. The fifth stanza of this work is quoted by Perasiriyar in his comment on Sutra 113 of the prosody section of the Tolkappiyam, and ascribed, probably by mistake, to Bhutattar. How the mistake arose it is difficult to say. One explanation seems possible. The two Alvars were so closely associated with each other and their works were so similar both in form and matter, as in the *Prabandhams* they most assuredly are, that the great commentator fell into error "nodding" like great *Homer* himself.

THESE EARLY ALVARS BELONG TO THE SECOND CENTURY A. D.

Then arises the question whether he is the same as the Poygaiyar who celebrated the great Chola Sengan in the poem Kalavali "forty," another of the collection above referred to, and two poems in the Purananuru upon the Chera king Kok-Kodaimarban. On considerations of literary criticism this author is regarded as different. In one of the two poems in the Purananuru he says "our town is Tondi" referring to the Tondi of the Cheras.

The birth-place of Poygai Alvar is Kanchi, according to all accounts. Another explanation is perhaps possible for the statement, and that is that he was referring to the town of his patron, as his own out of regard for him or in mere compliment. In case the two authors should prove to be the same, the Poygaiyar who celebrated the Chola Sengan and released from prison his own patron, the Chera king, would fix the limit of time. In any case the difference is not likely to be many generations. The age of Poygai Alvar should be the age of the last Sangam. Whatever that be, the striking similarity between the *Kural* of Tiruvalluvar and Poygaiyar's *Innilai* would make him early in the age of the *Sangam*. I have discussed with the requisite fullness the question of the age of the *Sangam* in my book " The Beginnings of South Indian History ". I have not seen anything of evidence offered by my critics to change the position ; nor have my own further studies given me reason to change my views. The question still rests upon the synchronism established between the body of rulers of this period and Gaja Bahu of Ceylon. The new epigraphical light that comes from one of the Pandya grants goes so far only to confirm the conclusion I arrived at years ago. Still keeping an open mind upon the question and being constantly on the look out for substantial facts or reasons in support of any other period for the *Sangam*, I believe I am warranted in ascribing, in the present stage of research upon the question, the second century A. D. as the age of Poygai Alvar. The comment of Perasiriyar already quoted refers to the *andadi* verses of Poygaiyar and others, a description which implies the two others Bhutattar and Pey Alvar at any rate. This connection of the three is borne out by the similarity of style and sentiment, which is very close indeed, among the three *andadis*. We might then ascribe these early Alvars to the second century A. D. the age of Ilam Tirayan, Nalam Killi and Senguttuvan.

THE TRADITIONAL ORDER OF THESE SUPPORTED ON OTHER GROUNDS

We have already shown the reason for the principal inference, that at any rate, from the days of Ramanuja there came to be a recognised chronological order in regard to these Alvars and that it was recognised order which, with only one minor modification, was accepted by the hagiologists and handed down to us elaborated in the fashion it is in the guru-parampara. There is however an inscription of date 1118 and referring itself to the reign of Vikrama Chola, which specifies the ***Naksatra*** (asterism under which they were born) of two of the earliest Alvars, viz., Poygai Alvar and Bhutattu Alvar. The asterism is given as *Jyesta* (Tam. Kettai). According to the hagiologists these were born respectively in Sravana and Dhanista. This 'raises the question, how far the hagiologists are correct, and whether we should not prefer the inscription to the hagiologists. It is just possible that in this particular the hagiologists are wrong; but the question arises that in regard to this detail what better information the writer of the inscription could have had; the presumption would be the hagiologists put themselves to the trouble of investigating the matter when they set themselves up to write the lives of these saints. The inscription-writer could have been under no such obligation. He might simply have set down what he might honestly have heard about the matter either outside, or from the temple people. That after all is a 12th century piece of information in the inscription and could not lay claim to be accurate for centuries considerably anterior to the 12th century; whereas the information of the hagioiogists at least presumes an inquiry whatever might have been the sources of information available to them. In a matter like this there is not, perhaps, much to choose between the two, and it would be better to accept a perhaps continuous tradition rather than an isolated piece of information like the detail in the inscription relating to a period far anterior to the date of tne inscription. In any historical investigation into this matter the most reliable material would be the works of these saints themselves and where they differ from later information, the works have to be unquestionably preferred. On examining the works themselves the conclusion is borne in upon us, that the first Alvars, the three of them and Tirumalisai were the earliest in age, that age being the age of the *Sangam* celebrities. They all of them speak glorifying Vishnu *bhakti* (devotion to Vishnu) but at the same time they do regard Siva *bhakti* (devotion to Siva) with considerable sympathy, and make a visible effort to keep the Saivas in countenance. The earliest Alvars go the length even of describing Siva and Vishnu as one,[1] although they do recognise the united form as Vishnu. From this we advance one stage when we come to Nam Alvar. He is a little more of a Vaishnava and continues to regard these Saivas with sympathy no doubt, but does not generally give Siva the same pedestal that the earlier Alvars do. Tirumalisai coming between the two has something characteristic to say of the rivals, which is indicative of his attitude towards them. Tradition says that he proclaimed; ' we have learnt the religion of the Sakhya (Buddhism), we have

---

1. (1) அரன் நாரணன் நாமம் ஆன்விடை புள்ளூர்தி
உரைநூல் மறையுறையுங் கோயில்—வரைநீர்க்
கரும மழிப்பளிப்புக்கையது வேல்நேமி
உருவமெரி கார்மேனியொன்று.

First Andādi 5.

(2) ஒருருவனல்லை யொளியுருவம் நின்னுருவம்
ஈருருவ னென்பரிரு நிலத்தோர்—ஒருருவம்
ஆதியாம் வண்ணமறிந்தாரவர் கண்டீர்
நீதியால் மண்காப்பார் நின்று.

Second Andādi 60.

(3) தாழ்சடையும் நீண்முடியும் ஒண்மழுவும் சக்கரமும்
சூழரவும் பொன்னாணும் தோன்றுமால்—சூழும்
திரண்டருவி பாயும் திருமலைமேலெந்தைக்கு
இரண்டுருவு மொன்றாயிசைந்து.

Third Andādi 63.

learnt the religion of the Sramana (Jainisim), we have examined the Agama of Sankaranar (Saiva Agama) ; but by fortunate good luck we have come to rest our faith in the Black One with red-eyes and got rid of all that is evil. There is hereafter nothing impossible to us.[1] This is a fugitive piece, the value of which, as evidence, might be doubted; but the same idea is found repeated almost in identical terms but far less aggressively in stanza 6 of his work "Nanmugan Tiruvandadi". This stanza says, " the Sramanas are ignorant, the Bauddhas have fallen into delusion, the followers of Siva are unknowing innocents and those that will not worship Vishnu are low people indeed.[2] Similar sentiment, but identifying Siva with Vishnu is found scattered through the works of Nam Alvar. In one of his poems already referred to above he makes reference to the

---

1. சாக்கியங் கற்றோம் சமண்கற்றோமச்சங்கரனார்
ஆக்கியவாகம நூலாராய்ந்தோம்—பாக்கியத்தால்
செங்கட் கரியானைச் சேர்ந்தியாந்தீதிலோம்
எங்கட் கரியதொன்றில்.

2. அறியார் சமணரயர்த்தார் பௌத்தர்
சிறியார் சிவப்பட்டார் செப்பில்—வெறியாய
மாயவனை மாலவனை மாதவனை யேத்தாதார்
ஈனவரே யாதலாலின்று.

detailed items of worship, and refers distinctly to Adiyar and Bhagavar,[1] possibly indicating the existence of Siva Bhaktas along with Vishnu Bhaktas. In the "ten" from which the above is one, he breaks out into a hymn of thanks giving for the success of the propagation of *bhakti* to Vishnu, by means of which the earth was rid of the evil, Kali.[2] On the basis therefore of the development of the struggle of the school of *bhakti* and *bhaktas* against Buddhism and Jainism, the age of these, Bhaktisara and Nam Alvar, ought to follow immediately that of the first Alvars. Madhurakavi's work in the *Prabandham* is only 11 stanzas on devotion (bhakti) to his guru and does not come into general line sufficiently for criticism of this kind; but he places himself in intimate connection with Nam Alvar as his disciple, and in ordinary fairness as critics we ought to concede him the honour. In Kula-

---

1. See verse quoted in note 2 p. 25.

2. திரியும் கலியுகம் நீங்கித்தேவர்கள் தாமும்புகுந்து
பெரிய கிதயுகம்பற்றிப் பேரின்ப வெள்ளம் பெருக
கரியமுகில் வண்ணனெம்மான் கடல்வண்ணன் பூதங்கள்
[மண்மேல்
இரியப்புகுந்திசைபாடி எங்குமிடங் கொண்டனவே:
Tiruvāymoḷi. V. 2. 3.

sekara we do reach a very high stage of enthusiastic devotion to the god of his heart. Almost the same might be said of Periyalvar and his daughter, and these would follow Satakopa on this basis; but when we pass to Bhaktangrirenu we see a pronounced attitude of hostility to the Bauddhas and Jainas; one may trace a hostile reference to the Saivas[1] also. Yogivaha or Tiruppan has only 10 stanzas in the *Prabandham* which give us hardly a hint of his personality; and in Tirumangai Alvar, the last of them, it is possible to detect occasional reference to the inferiority of Siva in his grace-bestowing quality to Vishnu, but of pronounced hostility to the Saivas, there is perhaps not very much. He goes out of his way to celebrate the early Chola King Ko-Sengan in 10 stanzas celebrating Tirunaraiyur, wherein he even makes the statement

---

1. புலையறமாகி நின்றபுத்தொடு சமணமெல்லாம்
கலையறக் கற்றமாந்தர் காண்பரோகேட்பரோதாம்
தலையறுப் புண்டுசாவேன் சத்தியங் காண்மின் ஐயா
சிலையினா லிலங்கை செற்ற தேவனே தேவனாவான்

வெறுப்பொடு சமணர் மிண்டர் விதியில் சாக்கியர் கணின் [பால்
பொறுப்பரியனகள் பேசில் போவதே நோயதாகி
குறிப்பெனக் கடையுமாகில் கூடுமேல் தலையையாங்கே
அறுப்பதே கருமங்கண்டா யரங்கமா நகருளானே.

First Thousand: Tirumālai 7 and 8.

that he (Sengan) built 70 temples to Siva. This Chola king is one of the recognised Adiyars of Siva, and the miracle which Siva performed in connection with him comes in for frequent allusion both in Sambandar and Appar, the two Tevarm hymners of the early 7th century. After all there may be a considerable amount of personal equation in this matter and this alone cannot be held to be decisive of age.

OTHER CRITERIA OF AGE

There are other criteria, however of perhaps a more reliable character, by means of which, we can fix the age of some of these. We have already pointed out the reasons why Nam Alvar could not be referred to the 10th century. There is one more point which might be considered quite decisive. He celebrates the temple Tiruppernagar, ordinarily called "Koviladi", now in the Tanjore district. There is in the first stanza of the ten, the statement that Tiruppernagar is on the southern bank of the Ponni (Kaveri).[1] Tiruppernagar is,

1. திருமாலிருஞ் சோலைமலை யென்றேனென்னத்
திருமாலென்னெஞ்சு நிறையப்புகுந்தான்
குருமா மணியுந்து புனல் பொன்னித்தென்பால்
திருமால் சேர்விடம் தென் திருப்பேரே.

Tiruvāymoḻi. X. 8. 1.

I am informed, actually on the northern bank of the Kaveri and the southern bank of the Coleroon. The only explanation possible for this discrepancy is that in his days the Coleroon was known as the Kaveri, as it must have been, because the two branches into which the Kaveri divides itself as it strikes the island of Srirangam reunite at the southern end of the island. What was the Kaveri perhaps took off a little way below from the main river; the channel now known as the Kaveri is called in the locality Solan Kaveri; and according to the Kongudesa Rajakkal the channel of the Kaveri was constructed by Aditya, the Karikala Chola, son of Vijayalaye and father of the great Chola Parantaka. His time would be between Varaguna Pandya 867-68 and Parantaka 907. If Nam Alvar located this place on the southern side of the Coleroon and called the river Kaveri, he must have lived before him. We have therefore to look for him much earlier, and the test applied in the previous paragraph perhaps holds good in his case. We ought therefore to look for Nam Alvar at a time when the ***bhaktas***, both of Vishnu and Siva were coming into prominence, and when the work of these ***bhaktas*** was beginning to tell upon those people that were following the persuasion of the Buddha and Jina.[1] About the 5th century A. D. would seem the most suitable time for him, and stylistic and literary criticism would support this view.

The main part of his work is called Tiruvaymoli. This name, some ascribe to formation by analogy, as the Saiva work of Manikkavasagar was called Tiruvasagam, implying the posteriority of the Alvar to the Saiva saint. In truth the name Tiruvaymoli means the Veda. The Paripadal distinguishes "Vaymoli" (the Veda) from "Marai" (the Upanishads).[2] In fact the latter is called "Vedattumarai.[3]" Tirumangai

1. வணங்கும் துறைகள் பலபலவாக்கி மதிவிகற்பால்
பிணங்கும் சமயம் பலபலவாக்கி அவையவைதோ
றணங்கும் பலபலவாக்கிநின் மூர்த்தி பரப்பிவைத்தாய்
இணங்கு நின்னோரையில்லாய் நின் கண்வேட்கை
[யெழுவிப்பனே.

Tiruviruttam 96.

2. மாயாவாய்மொழியுரைதர வலர்ந்து
வாய்மொழி யோடை மலர்ந்த
தாமரைப்பூவினுட் பிறந்தோனுந்தாதையும்
நீயெனமொழியுமாலந்தணரருமறை. [III. ll. 11-14.

3. வேதத்துமறை நீ பூதத்து முதலுநீ.

Ibid l. 66.

Alvar[1] seems to support this difference in the use of the terms.[2] Satakopa himself seems to let us into the secret in stanzas 64 and 94 of his Tiruviruttam.[3] In the first he he implies that he was putting in Tamil what the "gods of the earth" have put in "Riks" (verse) and likens his effort to people bitting at tender fruit for lack of the ripe one. In the other he says that it is only "Vaidikas" (those that follow the path of the Veda) that are

---

1. வாயோதுவேதம் மல்கின்ற தொல்சீர்
மறையாளர்நாளும் முறையால் வளர்த்த
தீயோங்க வோங்கப்புக ழோங்குதில்லைத்
திருச்சித்ரகூடம் சென்று சேர்மின்களே.

Periya Tirumoḻi. II. 2. 2.

2. இருக்கிலங்கு திருமொழிவா யெண்டோளீசற்கு
எழில்மாட மெழுபது செய்துலகமாண்ட
திருக்குலத்து வளச்சோழன்.

Ibid. VI. 6. 8.

3. இருக்கார்மொழியால் நெறியிழுக்காமை உலகளந்த
திருத்தாளிணைநிலத்தேவர் வணங்குவர் யாமுமவா
ஒருக்காவினையொடும் எம்மொடும் நொந்துகனியின்மையில்
கருக்காய் கடிப்பவர்போல் திருநாமச்சொல் கற்றனமே.

மைப்படிமேனியுஞ் செந்தாமரைக்கண்ணும் வைதிகரே
மெய்ப்படியாலுன் திருவடி சூடும் தகைமையினார்
எப்படி யூராமிலைக்கக் குருட்டாமிலைக்கு மென்னும்
அப்படியானுஞ்சொன்னேன் அடியேன் மற்றுயாதென்
[பனே

qualified to sing in glory of Vishnu, but he has also attempted doing so in Tamil very much like the blind cow that joins in the frolics of the seeing one. The name apparently goes back to antiquity which would make imitation of Manikkavasagar impossible. In the absence of similar authoritative precedent, the name Tiruvasagam may reasonably be argued as having been formed by analogy from the *Tiruvaymoli.*

We have given reasons enough to show that Kulasekhara must have followed perhaps early in the 7th century or late in the 6th. For Periyalvar we have got the lead from himself. He refers to two personages, one of them an officer of some influence in the court of the Pandya and attached to the temple of Tirukkottiyur. The Alvar refers to him twice in the course of his works and on both occasions exhibits great regard for him as a devotee of Vishnu,[1] but that does not lead us very far. In another connection he refers to a certain

---

1. அல்வழக்கொன் றுமில்லா
வணிகோட்டியர்கோ னபிமானதுங்கன்
செல்வனைப்போலத் திருமாலே
நானு முனக்குப் பழவடியேன்.

Pandya king whom he calls Nedu Maran.[1] In yet another connection[2] he refers in general terms to the Pandaya who set up the fish emblem on the Himalayas. These two attributes are given to the Pandya who forms the subject of the modern illustrative stanzas of the Tamil grammar Iraiyanar Ahapporul. I have for good reasons[3] identified that Nedu

---

நளிர்ந்தசீலன் நயாசலன்
அபிமானதுங்கனை நாடொறும்
தெளிந்த செல்வனைச் சேவகங்கொண்ட
செங்கண்மால் திருக்கோட்டியூர்
குளிர்ந்துறைகின்ற கோவிந்தன்
குணம் பாடுவாருள்ள நாட்டினுள்
விளைந்த தானியமு மிராக்கதர்மீது
கொள்ளகிலார்களே.

I. 1. 11 & IV. 4. 8.

1. மன்னர் மருக மைத்துனன்மார்க்கொரு தேரின்மேல்
முன்னங்குநின்று மோழை யெழுவித்தவன் மலை
சொன்னவில் கூர்வேற் கோன் நெடுமாறன் தென்கூடற்
[கோன்
தென்னன் கொண்டாடுந் தென்திருமாலிருஞ் சோலையே.

IV. 2. 8.

2. பருப்பதத்துக் கயல் பொருத்த பாண்டியர் குலபதிபோல்
திருப்பொலிந்த சேவடி யென் சென்னியின்மேற்பொறித்
[தாய்
மருப்பொசித்தாய் மல்லடர்த்தாய் என்றென்றுன் வாசகமே
உருப்பொலிந்த நாவினேனை யுனக்குரித்தாக்கினையே.

V. 4. 7.

3. Pp. 258-70 of Beginings of South Indian History.

Maṛan with No. 2 of the genealogical table based on the Velvikkudi grant in the report of the government Epigraphist for 1906. The only other possibility is the Nedu Maran his grandson and contemporary of Sambandar. That would bring him to be almost a contemporary with Kulasekhara. Tirumangai Alvar stands out clear by his reference to (Dantidurga) Vairamegha as the overlord[1] for the time being of the ruler of Kanchi. There is another peculiar reference in his clebration of Srirangam ; he there speaks of a miracle that Vishnu performed of accepting the Tondaman (the Pallava ruler) as his devotee, and teaching him the secret "mantra,"[2] an act of beneficence

---

1. See the verse quoted in note 24. p.
Periya Tirumoḻi II. 8. 10.

2. துளங்குநீள் முடியரசர் தம்குருசில்
தொண்டை மன்னவன் றிண்டிறலொருவற்கு
உளங்கொளன்பினோ டின்னருள் சுரந்து
அங்கொருநாழிகை லேழுடனிருப்ப
வளங்கொள்மந்திரம் மற்றவர்க்கருளிச்
செய்தவாரடியே னறிந்துலக
மளந்த பொன்னடியேயடைந்துய்ந்தேன்
அணிபொழில் திருவரங்கத் தம்மானே.

Periya Tirumoḻi V. 8. 9.

generally stated to have been done by Vishnu in connection with Tirumangai Alvar himself. I have not been able to find out exactly what this means, but expect to be when next time I am able to visit the temple Paramesvara Vinnagaram in question. Thus then the age of the Alvars as a class lies between somewhere about the commencement of the 3rd century A D. and the 9th century; most of the Saiva Adiyars being referable also to about the same time. It is impossible to make any further elaboration of the subject on this occasion.

EVIDENCE OF SECULAR LITERATURE

It will be clear from the above that the opinion formed by Sir R. G. Bhandarkar that Vaishnavism might have travelled to the South as early as the first century A. D. stands substantiated from Vaishnava literature; but there is fortunately for us secular literature which takes us further backward than this limit for which the earliest we have ascribed is the commencement of the 3rd century A. D. A work that was recently published by our veteran Pandit and Editor of the "Ancient Classics", Mahamahopadyaya V. Swaminatha

Aiyar Avergal, whose service to Tamil literature cannot easily be exaggerated, is what is called " Paripadal ", one of the eight famous classical collections, standing alongside of " Ahananuru " and " Purananuru ". The original work is supposed to have been composed of 70 poems of varying length of which the present edition brings out only 22 with portions of just a few more. Among those there are about seven relating to Vishnu. Of these, the authors are Ilam Peruvaludi, Kaduvan Ilaveyinan, Kirandaiyar, Nalleluniyar. These authors are, some of them, known by their works in other collections also, while some of them are known by their work in this. The greater part of the work available has the advantage of a commentary by, in several respects, the best of commentators, by name Parimel Alagar whose commentary on the Kural, is by common consent the best of all. He was one of those whose proficiency in both Sanskrit and Tamil was very great and equally so. In a commendatory verse regarding him this work Paripadal is referred to as the " nectar coming out of the ocean of the literature of the Sangam." He came of the family of worshippers of the Paramesvara

Vinnagaram temple (Ulahalanda Perumal temple) in Conjeevaram. The text of the poems devoted to Vishnu indicates in a fulness of detail, the mode of worship of the Pancharatra Agama, not to speak of other branches of Vaidika literature (not ordinarily to be expected in such sources). Poem III by Kaduvan Ilaveyinam states in detail the four vyuhas of the Pancharatrins, Vasudeva, Sankarsana, Pradhyumna, Aniruddha.[1] It further refers in detail to various of the doings of the child Krishna, thus indicating that the cult of Krishna and the Agamic work of the Pancharatrins alike had reached and had attained to considerable vogue, in the distant south (Madura) in the early centuries of the Christian era. Poem 15 by Ilam Peruvaludi which is devoted to Tirumalirunjolai states in clear terms that the temple there contained the images of Krishna and Baladeva. These are not to be found in the temple in the present day. It is not alone in this special work, that this worship is found described. Other Sangam works, like the Purananuru mention the divine character of Krishna and

1. செங்கட்காரி கருங்கண் வெள்ளை
பொன்கட்பச்சைப் பைங்கண்மால்.

Poem III lines. 81 and 82.

Baladeva in as clear terms.[1] Among the numbers of temples mentioned in a place like Kaveripattanam, capital of the Chola country, the Silappadhikaram refers to the temples of Krishna and Baladeva again.[2]

These references together would take us at least to the Sangam times, and the way that the details of the cult of Krishna are handled in these poems indicate that they were of considerably anterior vogue. We have already given a reference to the Saiva agama in dealing with Bhaktisara. We also qouted a reference to what seems meant for the Saiva Adiyars in Nam Alvar's work. These taken together

---

1. எற்றுவலனுயரிய வெரிமருளவிர் சடை
மாற்றருங்கணிச்சி மணிமிடற்றோனும்
கடல்வளர் புரிவளை புரையுமேனி
யடல்வெந்நாஞ்சிற் படைக் கொடியோனும்
மண்ணுறு திருமணி புரையும்மேனி
விண்ணுயர் பொற்கொடி விறல்வெய்யோனும்
மணிமயிலுயரிய மாறாவென்றிப்
பிணிமுகவூர்தி யொண்செய் யோனுமென
ஞாலங்காக்குங் காலமுன்பின்
றோலாநல்லிசை நால்வருள்ளும்.

Puram : poem 56 by Narkīrar.

2. வால்வளைமேனி வாலியோன் கோயிலும்
நீலமேனி நெடியோன் கோயிலும்.

V. 11-171 and 172.

make it clear that Vaishnavism of the agamic kind and Saivism were both prevalent in the Tamil land as long back as the age of the Sangam; the best part of it, to which these works relate cannot be brought very much this side of the commencement of the 3rd century.

I have pointed out in my book "The Beginnings of South Indian History"[1] that there are references to an invasion of the scuth by the Mauryas in some of the older poems of of the Sangam, and indicated that the opposition that was set up and maintained persistently against northern conquest had possibly in it an element of religion, the south standing up for orthodox Brahmanism as against the encroachment of Buddhism by the persuasive eloquence and persistent effort of the great Buddhist emperor Asoka. The Tamil literature of this period has references scattered all over to the colonies of Brahmans brought and settled down in the south, and the whole output of this archaic literature exhibits unmistakably considerable Brahman influence in the making up of that literature. It is impossible

[1] Ch. II.

within the limits of this paper to go into more detail on this interesting problem, but any casual reader of Tamil literature could see for himself the working of the northern Brahman and the southern Dravidian in a common effort at preserving Brahman orthodoxy against the encroachment of Buddhism.

It is fashionable criticism in certain quarters that Saivism had the allegiance of South India first of all and Vaishnavism came into the place as an interloper imitating Saivism and adapting itself to their clientele. A mere perusal of early literature gives the lie direct to this assumption. What was said of the Vaishnava literature of the Alvars, at any rate the great majority of them, in regard to the tolerance of Saivism is true perhaps in a slightly lesser degree of the Saiva Adiyars. Passing out of the age of the Sangam we come to the age of the Pallavas of the early rulers of whom, history has yet known but little. The dynasty of the Sanskrit charters called themselves Bhagavatas. When we come, however to the age of the great Pallavas, we find the two going together. Some scholars have made capital out of a passage in one of the Pallava inscriptions to an explicit reference to Saiva Siddhanta in connection with Narasimha Varman II.[1] But the same Pallava records refer to his great-grandfather Simha Vishnu in terms which leave no possibility of escape from regarding him as a Vaishnava.[2] Mahendra Varman built shrines both of Vishnu and Siva ; several of his cave-temples exhibit shrines to all the three Brahma, Vishnu and Siva. In the age of the Pallava domination, which followed immediately, both Vaishnavism and Saivism flourished ; Vaishnavas and Saivas on the one side wrangling and disputing againt the Bauddhas and Jainas : but so far the evidence of any systematic persecution is, at the very best, very slender. We pass from the age of the Pallavas to the age of the great Cholas among whom the rulers were

---

1. Teshāmvamśē prasūtādraṇa rasikapurōnmmarddanād Ugradaṇdāt
Subrahmaṇyaḥkumāraḥ Guha iva Parāmādiśvarādāttajanmā
Śaktikshuṇṇārivarggō vidita bohunayaśśaivasiddhāntamārggō
Śrīman Āṭyantakāmaḥ kshatasakalamalo dhūrdharaḥ Pallavānām
S. I In. I. 24. sl. 5 and 6.

2. Bhaktyārādita Vishṇuḥ Simhavishṇuḥ.
S. I. In. II. 74 l. 12. Udayēndiram Grant.

in the majority of cases Saivas; but, as with Indian sovereigns before them and after them, the persuasion of the individual monarch did not affect their patronage of all religions alike. It was in this particular age that Saivism and Vaishnavism alike hardened into sects with a systematised canonical literature; and it is the work of systematisation that emphasised the differences and brought into religious controversies a certain degree of acrimoniousness. Much the same state of things continued till some of the great aggressive Virasaiva sects came into existence. Even then the rulers of the kingdoms did their best to hold the balance even, despite considerable amount of ill-treatment of the weaker sects, and some possible destruction even of temples and buildings chiefly as a result of occasional outbreaks of popular fury. The empire of Vijayanagar came into existence under circumstances which did not permit of sectarian rancour being given vent to. The state therefore of tolerance and development in religion continued unbroken all through the history of Hindu India from almost Mauryan times in the distant south.

Before closing it would be just as well to indicate that if this outline of the history of

" Vaishnavism before Ramanuja" should stand the test of further criticism and make the chief landmarks in its history accepted by the world of scholars, several of the now accepted positions in literary and religious history of India even in regard to Sanskrit will have to be revised. All along I have advisedly kept from drawing in any Sanskrit evidence for the reason that it strikes me that several of the positions of a general character in respect of that literature may have to be modified. By way of illustration it may be pointed out that Dr. Schraeder[1] ascribes the Pancharatra Samhitas, to about A. D. 300. This position would cease to be tenable. Sir R. G. Bhandarkar himself in his book on Vaishnavism states that the cult of Rama came into vogue in the 11th or the 12th century. There is ample evidence to Rama being identified with Vishnu by the earliest of the Alvars. Kulasekhara gives a summary of the whole of the Ramayana as it is in his " ten " on Chidambaram. Much has been written about the coming in of the Krishna cult and of its importation into India by the Abhiras and of its

1. Intro. to Ahirbudhṇiya Samhita p. 99.

post-Christian character. It is at the very best doubtful whether this position could stand. There are various other lines of investigation such as the age of some of the Puranas, the Mahabharata, Manu &c., which this particular subject suggests, and it is to be hoped they will all get worked up satisfactorily in course of time so as to carry research work several, stages farther in respect of the history of " the literature and culture of India. "

ERRATA.

p. 3. l. 1. for Tirmalisai read Tirumalisaī

p. 5. l. 9. omit both the commas

p. 7. 3rd l. from bottom for Bhagavta read Bhagavata

p. 8. note l. 1. last for h read ḥ

l. 4. for pratīchu read pratīchī

l. 6. read Vāsudēvē=amalā'sayāḥ

p. 17. no. 1. for Poigai read Poygai.

p. 32. l. 2. delete comma.

p. 49. l. 7. delete comma after *and*.

l. 8. for gramatical read grammatical.

p. 50. l. 10. for forms read norms

note l. 1. insert ம் before மி.

p. 51. note l. 3. from bottom omit க்.

p. 63. note l. 2. for தோஓ read தோரு.

p. 64. l. 4. from bottom for philologists read philologist

p. 65. l. 2. from bottom for kshirabdi read kshirabdhi

p. 68. note last line read the first letter of the name. C instead of G.

p. 75. last line insert *this* between was and recognised.

p. 79. l. 6. close quotation after us.

p. 85. l. 7. for bitting read biting.

p. 88. l. 5. from bottom for clebration read celebration

note l. 1. for note 24. p. read note 1. p. 37.

p. 88. note 2 l. 2. for திண்டிறவொ read திண்டிறலொ.

" l. 4. for நாழிகைலேழு read நாழிகையேழு.

p. 89. last line for Mahamahop*adyaya* read *padhyaya*

p. 91. l. 8. for yinam read yinan

p. 95. note 1. l. 3. for bohu read bahu.

On p. 62 and the following pages for Yadhoktakari read Yathoktakari: Yadoktakari would be popular Tam. Yathoktakari Cor. Sans; the other being neither the one nor the other.

INDEX

Aḍiyārs of the Śaivas, born in the Tamil country exclusively 11
Aḍiyar and Bhagavar 80
Alankāra Sarvasva, commentary on, ... 32
Amudan, of Arangam (Śrīrangam) his centum on Rāmānuja, 17 ; of Śrīrangam, ... 22
Augustan age, the, of Tamil Liter, Bishop Caldwell's view, ... 4
Ābhīras, the, and the Krishna cult, ... 97
Āditya, the Karikāla Chola, ... 83
Āgamic, worship 8 ; Āgama, ... 9
Āḷavandār, 29, 58, 60 ; grandson of Nāthamuni, ... 46
Āḷvārs, the, Prof. Seshagiri Sastri's view of, 5 ; their birth places, 9 ; Āchāryas of the Vaishṇavas, born in the Tamil country, 11, 12 ; names of, dates when flourished, 13. Dr. Bhandarkar's view of them, 13 ; the works of, thrown into form, 16 ; the, and their order in the Prabandhasāram 38 ; the 1st (three), 67 ; the first three, their time, 75 ; the first three and Tirumaḷiśai... ... 77
Āḷvar Tirunagari, (Kurukai), ... 44
Ānaimalai, omission of, by Nam Āḷvār, examined. 56
Āndhrapūrṇa's Yatirājavaibhavam, quoted from, ... 2 f.n.
Ārsha, Tam Āriḍam, ... 71

Āscharyamanjari, ... 30

Āvūr, siege of, ... 69

Betel-leaves, reference to chewing of, in the Tiruvāymoḷi and Śilappadikāram ... 50

Bhāgavatam, the, 10 ; its date, ... 9

Bhāgavata Purāṇa, a verse from. quoted in Mukundamālā, 14; Kulaśēkhara's posteriority to, 27

Bhāgavatas, the, ... 94

Bhakti, (devotion) her two little ones Gnāna Vairāgya, 11 ; the Draviḍa country the land of the birth of, 11 ; associated with the south in the hist of Vaish ... 9

Bhaktāngrirēṇu, his attitude to other religions and sects 81

Bhaktisāra and Nam Āḻvar, 80 ; Tirumaḻiśai, his association with Kanchi on the one side and a Pallava ruler on the other 62 : and Śaiva Āgama, 92 ; and Toṇḍamān, Iḷandirayan comtemporaries, ... 63

Bhandarkar, Dr. 11 ; Sir R.G. 26, 38 ; His 'Vaishṇavism, Śaivism and minor Religions', 6, 7 ; his work, 12 ; on the Rama-cult, 97 ; on the school of Bhakti, ... 3

Bhāratavarsha, ... 8

Bhūtattār, ... 73

Brahminism, orthodox, in the south, ... 93

Brahmanism and Hinduism the revival of, ... 61

Buddhism and the emperor Aśoka, 93 ; and Jainism, 80

Caldwell, Bishop, his view of the origin of Vaishṇavism, 4, of the Augustan age of Tamil Lit : ... 4

Cholas, the, and their age, ... 95

Dantidurga (Vairamēgha) and Tirumangai Āḻvār ... 88
Daśarūpaka, 30; the author of the, his time, 30; ... 30
Dravida country, the, 8, 10;—Saints, the Divine wisdom of 5
Dvijanmavara, ... 35
Gaja Bāhu, ... 74
Gaṇapati Śastri Pandit, ... 30
Gangaikoṇḍachola: (or Rajēndra) ... 58, 59
Gñana, spiritual knowledge, ... 11
Gopinatha Rao, the late Mr, history of Vaishṇavism 6
Govindāchārya, Mr. A. his 'Divine Wisdom of the Drāviḍa Saints' 5
Gujarat, ... 10, 11
Guṇabhara reference to a, by Tirumaḻiśai Āḻvār ... 54
Guruparampara, twelve Āḻvārs acc. to, 12; from Vēdānta Dēśika back to Rāmānuja. 40
Hultzsch Dr. E. 35, ... 65
Iḷam Peruvaḻudi, 90, ... 91
Iḷam Tirayan, 69; Toṇḍamān, 63; Iḷandirayan (Tirayan) 70
India South, religions and sects compared by the Āḻvārs 79
Innes, Mr. L. C., his age of Māṇikkavāśagar ... 6
Innilai 72, 74
Iraiyanār Ahapporuḷ 87
Jagadēkamalla, 27; Pērmāḍi vassal of, ... 14
Jainism—and Buddhism, protests of, against Vedic Ritualism 4
Kaḍiyalūr Rudran Kaṇṇanār 63
Kaḍuvan Iḷaveyinan, 90, ... 91
Kaḷavaḷi 73

Kali age, the, ... 8
Karikāla Chola... 63, 69, ... 70
Kavibhūshaṇa, ... 32
Kānchi, occupation of, by an overlord of the Pallava F. N. 37
Kārīyāṛṛuttunjiya Neḍum Kiḷḷi 70
Karṇāṭaka 11
Keraḷa overlordship in South India 36
Kāṭṭumannārkoil 25
Kāvēri the, and the Coleroon at Śrīrangam ... 83
Kīrandaiyār 90
Kokkōdaimārban Chera in Puranānūru ... 73
Kōlambapura (Quilon) 32
Kolli (Quilon), 35 and Vanjūkulam wrongly equated. 26
Kongu, Kulaśēkhara ruler over 35
Ko-Śengan, Chola, ... 81
Kōḷi (Uraiyur the Chola capital) 35
Krishna cult, the, in Puranāṇūṛu and other Śangam works, 91; the cult of, and the Pāncharātra Āgama, 91; cult, the, in Śilappadikāram, ... 91
and Baladēva at Tirumālirunjōlai ... 91
Kūḍal (Madura) 35
Kulaśēkhara, 86; probable date of, 15; his date must be before 1088, 34; traditional incarnation of Kaustubha, 23; Quilon (Kolli) otherwise Tiruvānjikulam, birthplace of, 23; his oath on the honesty of Vaishṇavas, 24; and his devotion to his god, 81; his poems, 20; and the Rama cult, 97; anterior to Maṇakkal Nambi, 29; of Travancore, ... 31

Kulaśēkharānka 14
Kulaśēkharavarma of Mahōdayapura 30
Kulaśēkhara Nambi, of Mahōdayarpaṭṭinam, his lamp in the temple, ... 33
Kulaśēkharānka, id : with Kulaśēkhara Āḻvār ... 14
Kulōttunga Chola, record of his 18th year ... 33
Kuraḷ and Innilai, similarity between 74
Kūrattāḻvār 17
Kurukaikkāvalappankōvil 59
Kurukai 42
Lingapurāṇa apparent reference to, by Nam Aḻvar 49
Madras Review, the, ... 6
Madhurakavi, 18 ; his 11 stanzas on his Guru, 46 ; his contribution to the Prabandham literature, 45 ; the last of the Āḻvārs, how far true, 47 ; his teaching on the all necessary character of a guru, his 11 stanzas, Śaṭakopa his guru, 20 ; and Nam Āḻvār, 80 ; Āḻvār equated with the minister so named, examined. 47
Madhyadēśa, the orthodox 4
Madhvāchārya, Ānanda Tīrtha 27
Madhura and the Krishna cult 91
Mahāpūrṇa, guru to be sought 2
Mahārāshṭra, the 10, 11
Mahēndra Varman 95
Mahōdayapura, same as Vanjikuḷam ... 31
Malaimanḍalam 34
Malik Kafur, his invasion of the Tamil country ... 32

Maṇakkāl Nambi, 29, ... 34
Māṇikkavāśagar, the age of, by Mr. L. C. Innes, 6; his Tiruvāśagam, ... 84
Māran, son of Kāri, (Nam Āḻvār) 42
Māran Kāri, minister of an early Pāṇḍya king, ... 46
Maurya invasion of the south, the 93
Mukundamālā, 14, 25 34
Music, setting to, of poems 56
Muttoḷḷāyiram 71
Nāthamuni, 29, 46, 60; was he the direct disciple of Nam Āḻvār 47
Nalamkiḷḷi, 70; Chola, (otherwise, Śēṭ Chenni, Puṭpahai, Tērvaṇkiḷḷi) 69
Nalleḻuniyār 90
Nam Āḻvār, 18, 60, 78, his date, 41, 42, his inspiration from Vishṇu, 43; his pre-eminence, 19; his diction examined 48, and his grammar, 49, exposition of the various problems of life and religion, 54, was he of the 10th century 82, his unique position among the Āḻvārs, 22, and Śaiva Aḍiyars 92
Nandivarman, Pallava 37
Nānmugam Tiruvandādi 79
Nārada, the sage 10
Naregal. in Dharwar, temple, inscription in it ... 14
Narasimhavarman 36
Narasimha Varman II and Śaiva Siddhānta ... 95
Nāyanmārs, the, or the Śaiva saints 15
Nēḍu Māran Pāṇḍya 87

Nēḍu Māran, II, contemporary of Sambandar ... 88
Padma Purāṇā, the, on Śrimad Bhāgavatam ... 10
Padmaśara 35
Pagan, Inscription in, ... 33
Pallavas, the 36; their age. 94
Pāncharātra Āgama, the, ... 91
Paramēśvara Varman 65
Paramēśvara Viṇṇagaram 89
Parāntaka 59
Parāntaka Chola 36
Pārkkaḍal (Kshīrābdhi) 55
Parimēl Aḻagar, the Kuṛaḷ commentator ... 90
Paripāḍaḷ, ... 56
Paripāḍal, Ahanānūṛu and Puranānūṛu ... 90
Pāṭṭiyalmarabu, ... 72
Pattupāṭṭu 62
Perumbāṇāṛṛuppaḍai quoted 63
Pērāśiriyar 73
Pērāśiriyar (Mahāchārya). 70
Permaḍi of the Sinda dynasty, vanquished Kulaśē-kharāṅka 14
Periyāḻvār and his daughter 81; his time by internal evidence 86
Periyār 26
Perumāḷ Tirumoḻi, 25, ... 35
Perumbāṇāṛṛuppaḍai, of Rudran Kaṇṇanār ... 67
Pēy Āḻvār 64
Piḷḷān, the spiritual successor of Rāmānuja, 46; his order of the Āḻvārs in a śloka, his commentary on Tiruvāymoḻi 1000 19
Ponni, the, (the Kāvēri) 82

Poonamallee 33
Post-Christian character of the Krishṇa cult ... 98
Poygai Āḷvār 63; his date 70
Andādi,his 71; his Tiruvandādi 72
Poygai and Bhūtattu Āḷvārs, the asterism under which born Jyēshṭa or Kēṭṭai 76
Prabandha, the 91; when cast into its present form. 28
Pradyumnābhyudaya ... .28, 32
Puranānūṟu 69
Purāṇas, the, the Māhabhārata, Aham, and their ages, the investigation of 98
Raghavaiyangar, Pandit M. 6
Rahasyatrayasāram, the, of Vēdānta Dēsika ... 9
Rajagopalachariar, Prof. 6
Rāmānuja, 12, 60; his mission, 2; his work regarding the Prabandham, 17; the Āḷvārs previous to, 7; the preceding gurus, their succession according to Vedāntāchārya ... 21
Rāmānuja Nūṟṟandādi, 28; quoted from, F.N. 17, 18; and a recognised order of the Āḷvārs in, ... 37
Rāmāyaṇa, the, favourite work of Kulaśēkhara, ... 23
Ravivarman, Kulaśēkhara, sometimes called, Ravivarma bhūpa 32
Ravivarma dēva, and his pandits 32
Rivers, sacred, the, of the south 8
Saguṇa Brahmam as opposed to Nirguṇa ... 55
Śaivism 3
Samādhi, the, of Nathamuni 57
Sambandar and Appar, their reference to Ko-Śengaṇ, Chola 82
Samudrabandha 32

Śangam celebrities, the 77
Śangam, the last ... .74, 75
Sangrāmadhīra 33
Sanskrit evidence, abstention from drawing ... 97
Schraeder, Dr. on the Pāncharātra Samhitas ... 97
Śaiva sect, absence of acrimonions reference to the, examined... ... .51, 52
Śengaṇ Chola 73
Śenguṭṭuvan, Iḷam Tirayan, Nalam Kiḷḷi ... 75
Śen Tamiḻ 6
Seshagiri Sastri, M. Prof. 14
Śilappadikāram 50
Simha Vishṇu... 95
Śiva and Vishṇu as one 78
Śoḻan Kavēri 83
South Indian History, the Beginnings of ..74, 93
Srinivasa Aiyangar, Mr. M. his 'Tamil Studies.' ... 6
Śrīrangam, Kulaśēkhara going there after giving up royal life ... ... :4
Śrīvilliputtūr, omission of, by Nam Āḻvār and Tirumangai 55
Subhadrādhananjayam 30
Subrahmania Aiyar, Sir, Lectures, Mr. G. Rao ... 6
Sundaram Pillai, the late Mr., on Vaishṇava traditions 5
Mahamahōpadhyaya V. Swaminatha Aiyar ... 89
Tamraparṇi, the 8
Tanjore, Chola capital, ... 36
Tantra, 9, ritualistic basis of Vaishnavism, 1, ... 9
Tantraism, Vaishnavism diverged from ... 3
Tapatīsamvaraṇam 30

Tērkkiḷḷi, ... F.N. 67, 68
Ṭīkāsarvasva, commentary on the Amarakōśa ... 31
Tirayan ... ... F.N. 67, 68
Tirukkoṭṭiyūr and Abhimāna Tungan... ... 86
Tirukkōvalūr 64
Tiruppērnagar, or Koviladi 82
Tirumaḷiśai Āḷvār 67
Tiumaḷiśai Āḷvār, His Nānmugan Tiruvandādi quoted F. N. 3; between the earliest Āḷvārs and Nam Āḷvār 78
Tirumangai Āḷvar, 37, 81, ... 37
Tirunaraiyūr 81
Tirupati, Kulaśēkhara going to, ... 25
Tiruppāṇ Āḷvār 8
Tiruvāymoḷi, the recital of the, in Śrīrangām ... 52
Tiruvāymoḷi and Tiruvāśagam, argument on analogy between 84
Tiruvandādi, the first 71
Tiruviruttam of Śaṭakopa 85
Tolkāppiyam 70
Tondainādu 65
Tondamān, the Pallava ruler 88
Tondi of the Cheras 73
Travancore, ascendancy of, not possible after 900... 36
Trikshatrachūdāmaṇī 33
Udayanangai 42
Ulahaḷanda Perumāḷ temple at Conjeevaram ... 91
Upanishads, bases of Vaishṇavism 1
Uraiyūr, siege of 69
Vaḍakalai Vaishṇavas 21
Vaikunṭham 65

Vaikuṇṭha Viṇṇagar 66
Vairāgya, (negation of desire) a step to salvation, 8. 11
Vaishṇavism, 61 ; Definition of, 1, 2 ; history of 9 ; a living religion, 16 ; offspring of the school of Bhakti, 3 ; was it an interloper in the South 94
Vaishṇava Tradition, 16 ; history in 5
Vaishṇavism and Śaivism hardening into sects, 96 ; tolerance between, 94 ; as against the Bauddhas and Jainas 95
Varaguṇamangai, reference to in one of Nam Āḷvar's poems, was the name derivative of Vāraguṇapāṇḍya ? 53
Vāymoḷi and Maṛai, the Vēda and the Upanishads. 84
Vēdāntachārya 21
Vēdanta Dēsika, quoted, F. N. 25 ; the scholar, his Tamil Prabandham, 20 ; his Rahasyatrayasāram, 9 ; his Prabandhasāram, 38 ; Adhikāra Sangraha, quoted from, F. N. 19
Vēgavatī, near Kānchipuram 32
Vehkā 63, 64
Vehkā, (Yathōktakari temple) 67
Vēḷvikkuḍi Grant, the 88
Vēnkaḍam 64
Vikrama Chola, the inscription referring to ... 76
Viṇṇagaram 64
Vijayanagar, the empire of 96
Vīra Nārāyaṇapuram 57
Vīra Nārāyaṇa Chola, (or Parāntaka I) ... 58
Vīraśaiva sects, the 96

Vishṇu, the chief guru, 19; associated with Śri, or Lakshmī supreme 2, ... 19
Vishṇu Bhakti, from the North, 12 Bhaktas in the Tamil land, 12; and Siva Bhakti, 77; getting rid of Kali 80
Vyangya Vyākhya 30
Vyūhas, the four, of the Pāncharātrins ... 91
Worship with flowers, incense etc., Purāṇic or Āgamic? 50
Yāpparuṇgalam, commentary of 67
Yathoktakāri 62, 63
Yogivāha, or Tiruppāṇ Āḻvār 80